Colton

History of a Staffordshire Village

Researched and written by
Gill Sykes and Shirley Carter (founder members)
Dorothy Bradbury (society member)

Illustrations compiled by
Bill Brown (society member)

Published by
Colton History Society

Printed by The Benhill Press Ltd., Brook Square, Rugeley, Staffordshire WS15 2DU

2008

ISBN 978-0-9558226-0-5

Contents

COLTON - THE HISTORY OF A STAFFORDSHIRE VILLAGE

INTRODUCTION:

Three founding members of Colton History Society, Gill Sykes, Shirley Carter and Sonia Jenkinson shared a desire to understand more about the history of their village, realising that unless first hand information from local villagers regarding the past century was collected and collated this would be lost forever.

It was decided to hold a meeting to see if other villagers would be interested in forming a Colton History Society. After an initial meeting on October 7th 2002 when a lot of interest was shown it was agreed that the Society would be formed and initially look back over the past 100 years.

Villagers have over the past five years shown an enormous interest and supplied the Society with hundreds of very interesting old photographs, scrap books with press cuttings and verbal recollections.

One of the inspirations for this book was a history written and published in 1897 by the then Rector of Colton, Reverend F. Parker, entitled "Colton and the de Wasteneys". In this book our society has aimed at expanding Reverend Parker's work.

Acknowledgements

We are indebted to many Colton residents for the help they gave enabling us to produce this book. Hundreds of photographs have been made available by many people. Many memories have been recalled.

We would like to thank in particular:

Allan Lloyd for painstakingly proof reading the text for us.

Gay Lawrence for information about the origins of the name of Colton, information on Colton House and also being a prime mover in obtaining the lottery grant that allowed us to publish this book.

David Bradbury for information on Transport and photographs.

Bev Croft for information on Frederic Bonney and Jill Croft for information on the Second World War.

For photographs and the oral memories of Sam Jones, Peter Jones, Lil Redmand, Nev and Alma James, Nona Goring, Sheila Bergin, Keith Williscroft, Hilda Williscroft, and Dorothy Bradbury .

For access to the school records Mrs. Lavender (former head of the school), the trustees and governors of St. Mary's school.

Gwen Johnson and Ruth Williams for their father's press cuttings and photographs.

The family of Mary Cooper for press cuttings.

The Parr Family for their large collection of photographs.

Acknowledgements

The Norman family for photographs.

Tony Atkinson for his 'memories of an evacuee' and his photographs.

Bob Meeson for his advice on the plan of the original church.

Joan Anslow for her illustrations.

Thea Randell and the staff of the Stafford Record Office and the William Salt Library.

Staffordshire Education Department.

Local Heritage *initiative*

Chapter One

Geology and
early history of
Colton and its
surroundings

Geology and early history of Colton and its surroundings

Staffordshire is a county rich in natural mineral resources all of which have been exploited over time.

Colton lies in a central position in the county situated in the valley of the River Trent. The name Trent derives from a Celtic word meaning 'trespasser' suggesting a river liable to flooding. This flooding produces excellent grassland for the raising of animals, a factor that will have particular importance to the area over the centuries. Underneath this there is a layer of rocks of the Triassic period (248-206 million years ago) mostly made up of keuper red marl, which is rich in nutrients and provides the basis for a very fertile soil for growing crops. Outcrops of sandstone occur at certain points in this geological layer, which has provided sandstone for building over the centuries just as the red marl has provided fertilizer for the fields and the clay for brick making. Also occurring in the immediate area of Colton are pockets of sand and pebbles. These were carried into the area in the ice age. In these shingle beds the pebbles can be of all sizes up to as big as a football and can be of great use as aggregates for road building and building in general. Four of these stones sit at the corners of Colton Bridge. They are erratic stones totally different to the other older stone in the area and were carried here and deposited by ice.

The overall impression therefore of the immediate vicinity of Colton is that the village lies in a rich and fertile area with access to a number of natural and usable materials all of which have been exploited at one time or another.

Prehistoric Times

As the last Ice Age came to an end around 12,000 years ago, bands of hunters who had crossed over via the land link that had once connected Britain to the Continent, migrated across the land in pursuit of herds of animals. These Paleolithic people left little evidence in Staffordshire except for flint and bone tools and evidence of cave occupation around Thor's cave in North Staffordshire.

Steadily the climate began to warm up bringing with this change the spread of trees across the landscape. From around 9000 BC in the Mesolithic Age, people became hunter-gatherers taking advantage of the fruit, nuts, and fungi, wild cereals, fish and game that now flourished. They moved around setting up seasonal camps, evidence of which we have very close to Colton where skeletal remains from this period were found in a cave on Etching Hill, Rugeley some years ago.

In the Neolithic age around 4500BC farming practices spread across Europe from the Middle East. This eventually brought about the creation of permanent farming communities adopting ways of maintaining soil fertility and allowing for the development of crops and domesticated animals. New tools developed in this period and not only do we have examples of them in Staffordshire in finds such as axe and arrow heads but also by their use in the building of monuments.

These monuments were mainly to do with burial rituals and practices and took the form of burial mounds and chambers of which there are a number in Staffordshire. Also in recent years the crop marks of other Neolithic monuments have been discovered not too far from Colton in the Trent Valley. Two large causewayed enclosures at Mavesyn Ridware and Alrewas have been found. The perimeter of these was marked by a number of ditches. Also a wooden 'henge' a timber version of Stonehenge, has been discovered near Barton under Needwood.

Aerial photo of Castle Ring courtesy of Cannock Chase Mining Museum

The Bronze Age period in Staffordshire from around 2000BC is marked by changes in practices and the development of round barrows for burials of which again there is crop mark evidence in the Trent Valley. Of far greater significance however is the evidence of the development of settled Bronze age farmsteads. This led gradually to pressure beginning to build up to clear more and more land and as time went on competition for this land intensified. It is in this period that there is the development of the hill fort enclosures such as the one at Castle Ring on Cannock Chase; the largest hill fort in Staffordshire and one of the largest in

England. Whether these forts were for show and prestige or for defence is not clearly understood as yet. They could possibly have been used for huge tribal gatherings or for protection in times of danger.

The Celtic peoples living in the vicinity at this time were probably from the Cornovii tribe known to be one of

This is a recreated Iron Age settlement at St. Fagans Museum in Wales. Photo courtesy of the museum

the three tribes in and around Staffordshire. The first evidence we have of habitation in Colton is from this period of the Iron Age. On a farm in Colton, evidence has been found of Iron Age Burnt Mounds. These are discarded mounds of rocks split obviously by the application of heat. It is not known exactly what these were used for but it has been suggested they could have been for cleaning and curing animal skins or for some cooking process.

In this iron age period people lived in small settlements in round huts made of mud, wood and straw for the roof. The settlement would usually be protected by a ditch and a wooden palisade or wall. This was to keep out wild animals such as wolves as much as a defence against attack. They would live in large family units all sharing the same space. There is much evidence that during the Iron Age more and more land was brought into cultivation and that many of the field systems that existed for centuries were organised during this time.

Roman Times

The Romans invaded Britain in A.D.43. They advanced through this area of Staffordshire in their attempts to push the hostile British tribes westwards. The Roman general Publius Ostorius Scapula established a base at Letocetum, the modern day Wall near Lichfield. This soon became a fort on a strategic Roman route cutting through Staffordshire linking London with the huge Roman centre at Wroxeter - Watling Street, the modern day A5. A second fort, not too far from Colton, was at Rocester near Uttoxeter. Other major Roman roads also crossed through this part of Staffordshire.

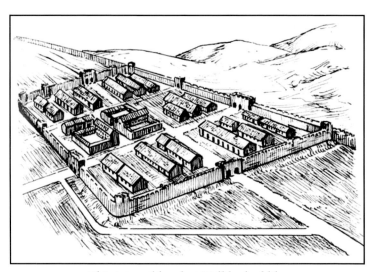

This is possibly what Wall looked like

We have little evidence of any impact by the Romans on the local population. Local people were obviously attracted to the civil settlements that grew up near the forts supplying the garrisons with goods and services. The civil settlements of Lichfield and Rocester both out lasted the forts when the

Romans finally withdrew from Britain and went on to flourish into a later period.

Once the Romans withdrew the British tribes were left to their own devices and gradually many of the Roman structures both physical and civil broke down. As the Romans quit they left behind them many mercenaries from Europe who settled here. It was not long before other invaders from mainland Europe, the Angles, Saxons and Jutes; arrived. They were coming from countries where land was very much under pressure and were attracted by the seemingly empty spaces of England. So began another invasion although this one was over a longer period of time.

Chapter Two

Colton in the

Anglo Saxon Period

Colton in the Anglo Saxon Period

With the abandonment of Britain by the Romans as their Empire disintegrated, the Anglo Saxons commenced their steady invasion of England. There was no cohesive enough structure amongst the British peoples for them to be able to defend themselves and resist these Anglo Saxon attackers and between 450 and 600AD the Anglo Saxons took over most of the area which corresponds to modern England.[1]

The Angles and Saxons invaded what eventually became the county of Staffordshire in the late sixth century. We now believe that the Angles probably entered this part of Staffordshire via the Humber estuary and then along the River Trent and that the Saxons first came into England from the south and the south east, pushed northwards and met with the Angles in this part of the Midlands.

It is now thought that the main British tribe facing the Anglo Saxons in this area of the Trent valley, which includes Colton, as we have already noted were probably the Cornovii Tribe. It is quite likely that the invaders once they had settled intermixed with the native peoples so that their eventual integration was relatively peaceful.

How Colton got its name

We know for certain that Colton was a settlement in Anglo Saxon times but not when it came into being. The origin of the name Colton is shrouded in mystery but probably dates to this period. There are a number of options to choose from. As settlements were often named by their most marked characteristic, then the Martlin Hill is the feature that most dominates Colton. There is no doubt that the "col" in Colton and neighbouring Colwich are the same, possibly derived from an early possessor "Cola" or the old Norse "Colla" even Latin "collis" both meaning "hill". Ton in Saxon times would have been a settlement or town. Therefore Colton was the town/settlement at the neck or bottom of the hill. Another theory is that the settlement belonged to a Saxon thegn known as Cola. Less likely are Coal Town where coal was found or Colt Town where colts were bred or even "Cola" the old English name for charcoal for there is certainly evidence that charcoal burning went on around the village.

The Founding of Mercia

A leader called Penda brought all the tribes together in this midland area to form the single Kingdom of Mercia with his capital at Tamworth close to the main Roman arterial routes of Watling Street and Ryknild Street.

What we now know as Staffordshire was part of this Kingdom of Mercia but it did not emerge as a defined area until much later. Mercia was at the height of its power amongst the Anglo Saxon kingdoms during the reign of Offa, King of Mercia (757 to 796). The earliest written record we have of Mercia is from the Venerable Bede in his book recording the History of The English Speaking People in the 8th Century. He noted that the River Trent divided the Kingdom into North and South with what he estimated to be 7,000 households in the north and 5,000 in the South. We have no way of knowing how true this was.

Religion

The early Anglo Saxons were Pagans who worshipped the many gods they believed were in the natural world all around them.

Christianity came to Staffordshire in 653 when Peada, king of Mercia, accepted Christianity in order to marry the daughter of the Christian King of Northumbria. After his conversion Peada brought to Staffordshire four Celtic missionaries to convert his people.

One of these was St. Chad who was appointed Bishop of the Mercians in 669 with his religious centre being established at Lichfield. In 822 Bishop Ethelweald established a Cathedral there where there has been one ever since. Christianity arrived in Colton sometime in this period because we know a priest lived in the settlement.

The late 7th Century saw the beginning of the practice of land being given by the wealthy to the church. Ethelbert King of Mercia gave land for a nunnery at Hanbury and established his neice Werburgh as an abbess there also with the responsibility of smaller houses at Blithbury on the boundary of Colton and Whiteladies at Brewood. An Abbey was founded on land given at Burton. Over the centuries Burton Abbey became very powerful through its acquisition of land in this part of Staffordshire. Abbots Bromley was one of its land holdings.

What life might have been like in Colton in Anglo Saxon times

Not a lot is known about how people lived in this period because there are very few written records and those that exist are for the later period.

An excavated site in Staffordshire in the Trent Valley at Catholme gives some clues as to what an Anglo Saxon settlement such as Colton may have been like.

Reconstruction of an Anglo Saxon settlement at "Bede's World" Museum.

The settlements appear to have been made up of a small group of single storey houses now called "hall houses" with smaller buildings nearby. The hall house would have been surrounded by an organised fenced or hedged farmyard and this appears to have made up the basic unit for one family grouping. A settlement would normally be a small hamlet consisting of a few of these individual farmsteads clustered together, laying the basis for what eventually became the village in medieval times. All the buildings would have been made of timber with a deep thatch roof and a door and window opening probably covered by shutters of some sort to keep out the wind and cold.

There would have been a central hearth with a hole in the thatch to let the smoke out. This structure would house the whole of one extended family.

The smaller buildings that surrounded these houses appear to have been mainly used for workshops. From animal bone evidence the animals they kept appear to have been mainly sheep, but also cattle, pigs and horses.

The settlements were surrounded by cultivated fields which in the earlier period were square or rectangular and are known as "Celtic fields" because they appear to have existed in this form well before the Anglo Saxons arrived. It would seem that for some centuries these fields were ploughed probably by one man using a wooden "ard" that cut a simple shallow furrow. The crops they grew appear to have been barley, oats, wheat, rye, beans, peas and flax.

What might people have worn

Evidence of the type of clothes they wore has been found from the excavation of burial sites. Fragments of materials have been retrieved and also metal dress fittings which indicate how the clothes were secured. The robe or tunic gathered at the waist was the common garment for a man, completed by hose and shoes. A woman wore a robe or dress that extended to her feet. The garments were usually linen and woollen. Natural vegetable colourings could produce a range of strong and cheerful hues with bright reds, greens and yellows. Brooches were used to fix clothing by the wealthy and the poor and amulets of stones and gold torcs (necklaces) were worn by the more wealthy.

Landholdings and those who worked them

The King had the allegiance of earls and lords or thegns in return for land. They were regarded as freemen and lived on larger estates farming a minimum of five hides. A hide was a unit of land measurement thought to be about 120 acres and was defined by the amount of land it was considered necessary to provide the living for one family.

Below the thegns but still regarded as a freemen were the ceorls. They farmed less than 5 hides but could still be quite wealthy. In return for the land and protection they had to work so many days for the local lord and give service in time of battle.

Below these two classes came the slaves. Much depended on this unpaid workforce and slaves were a prized item and there was a huge trade in them. People were enslaved from all parts of Europe and Africa and were usually taken in raiding parties and battle and sold in markets everywhere. Many of the Britons would have become slaves when the Anglo Saxons invaded and once a slave your descendants were born into slavery.

Life consisted of hard physical labour for these lower social groupings but from the examination of skeletons they appear to have been, on the whole, quite healthy. Surprisingly they were as tall as we are today which suggests their diet was good except in the periods of famine and pestilence that occurred on a fairly regular basis.

By the turn of the millennium England was able to support a population of at least a million because enough land was in good, cultivated condition to provide food of sufficient quality. Their food would have been totally organic and grown on a communal basis for the practicality of working the fields at the various seasons in the year.

Men were considered mature at 14 and women were often married by the time they were 12, often to older men. Skeletal evidence shows that they tended to live into their early 40's and you were very old if you survived into your 50's. The language that developed through integration became known as "Englisc" – a tongue that was spoken to a rhythm and contained many words we can recognise. Computer analysis of the English language as spoken today, shows that the hundred most frequently used words, words such as the, is, you; are all of Anglo Saxon origin.

The creation of Staffordshire

As time went on the larger kingdoms such as Mercia became divided into "Shires" and each shire was divided up into smaller units that became known as "Hundreds" In Staffordshire there were 5 hundreds created. Each shire had a representative of the King called the Shire Reeve, who eventually became known as the "Sheriff".

Danish Invasions

Life in Anglo Saxon England was seriously disrupted by the Danish invasions of the 9th and 10th Centuries. The Danes put an end to Mercian supremacy. In this part of the midlands they based themselves at Repton and subdued the surrounding area destroying Tamworth in the process in 874. They were finally checked by King Alfred of Wessex who prevented them from invading the whole of England. An area of England was created under Danelaw with its boundary marked by Watling Street; the Danes holding all land to the east of it and Alfred controlling the rest. Colton was on the borders of Danelaw.

Alfred had great influence over all parts of England and his legacy was huge. He devised an array of reforms and innovations that were to give decisive identity to the country that at his death was known as "Engla-lond"

Mercia reorganised it defences against the Danes in the early 10th century and it was during this period the Anglo Saxons fortified Stafford and Tamworth was recaptured. Most of the burghs (towns) around the country were fortified against future Danish attacks. Legend has it that a massacre of Danes took place near Marchington.

What We Know about Colton

We can deduce something about Colton in the Anglo Saxon period from Colton's entry in the Domesday Book. Although Domesday was a record compiled for King William after the Norman invasion of England in order to record the holdings of the Norman Knights he had rewarded for their support, it also encapsulates something of what Colton was like immediately prior to the Norman invasion.

The first entry shows that before the Conquest an Anglo Saxon called Almund had held it "Almund held it; he was free". The land holding was "1 hide". We have no way of knowing whether he was a thegn or a coerl. The size of the holding suggests that he was a Coerl because there are fewer than 5 hides but he may have held land elsewhere. We think this holding was the area around most of the present day village and over towards Admaston. A priest is also recorded in this entry. We have no idea whether there was a church. Often there would be a preaching cross in the open air where religious ceremonies were held and the priest would live in the village. Religion was very important to everybody because people believed that God intervened actively in daily life and one function of worship was to secure divine intervention on your own behalf. The priest therefore would be a very important member of the community.

He would probably be married and as well as his religious duties he would also take part in the services required from the villagers such as ploughing. There are only 30 priests recorded in Staffordshire in Domesday so it does suggest that Colton was a place of some significance to have its own priest. It is recorded in Frederic Parker's book "Colton and the de Wasteneys[2] that whilst laying out the gardens for Bellamour Lodge some skeletons were unearthed in the field known as "Chapel Yard" (now part of Bellamour Lodge Garden). This is close to the stream, often the site for Anglo Saxon churches and the bones could possibly have been evidence of an Anglo Saxon cemetery for the settlement. However this is all conjecture as all the physical evidence to verify our facts has been lost.

The second entry states "there is ½ hide… Aelmar held it" Again Aelmar was probably a coerl and there is evidence that this was the holding that later became known as Little Hay Manor on land that went from the upper part of High Street.

The final entry records "1 hide… Oda and Wulfric held it; they were free". Again they would possibly have been ceurls. It also records a mill that was there in Saxon times and was a very valuable asset. We now know this was a water mill based on the Trent where the Colton road crosses to Rugeley. This holding was based on the land that became Colton Hall Manor situated around the Martlin Hill and down to the banks of the River Trent.

All this evidence suggests that Colton comprised of three farmsteads and a water mill owned and worked probably by ceurls and their slaves. Five Slaves are included in the Domesday record and had probably been taken over by the new lords. We have no idea actually how many people these farmsteads supported other than each one would have housed an extended family unit. From the values in the Domesday record these Colton farmsteads are worth more than most of those in the surrounding area and had the added value of a water mill. They also had a priest as an important member of the community. This suggests that on the eve of William's invasion Colton was quite a significant place in Anglo Saxon Staffordshire.

Notes

1.   A History of Staffordshire M. Greenslade & D. Stuart Publ. Phillimore 1998.

2.   Colton and the de Wasteneys Family. Rev. P. Parker Private Publ. 1879

Chapter Three

Colton in the

Norman Period

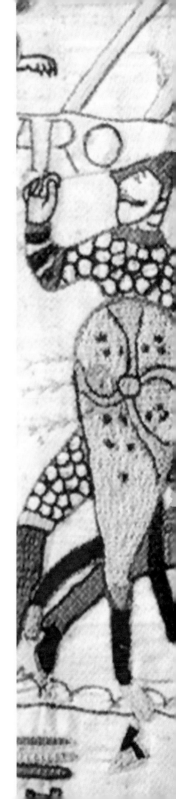

Colton in the Norman Period

What was Staffordshire like?

In 1086 when the Domesday Book was compiled for William I to show him what his new domain comprised of, Staffordshire was a poor county divided up between the lands belonging to the King himself, the church and a few of William the Conqueror's tenants in chief who had helped him at the Conquest.

Although Staffordshire was a large county there are comparatively few entries in the survey, suggesting that the 334 settlements recorded were thinly dispersed. Apart from a few areas in the south and along the central river system where many of the settlements were and where Colton is situated, there were extensive areas of forest which became out of bounds to all but the king, and upland, a lot of which was considered as waste. Subsistence agriculture would have predominated in most areas and even in the few towns trade was not of great significance. The town of Stafford had been the scene of one of the rebellions against William in 1069 which he had quickly and viciously put down. He then stamped his authority on the town and surrounding area in 1070 by building a castle there and destroying some of the houses.

An early Norman castle of the type that would have been erected by William I in Stafford.

William became the most important landowner in the county. He inherited the royal manors that had belonged to Edward the Confessor and also added the lands that had belonged to the Earls of Mercia such as Uttoxeter.

He valued his newly acquired kingdom by using the Anglo Saxon measurement of area known as "hides" and the whole county of Staffordshire was valued at only 500 hides.

Despite its poorness, there had been a good administrative and financial system established in Staffordshire in late Saxon times. The administrative system worked through areas known as 'hundreds' of which there were five in the county and it is clear that this system had existed for some time. The Hundreds were Seisdon in the south of the county, Offlow, Cuddlestone and Pirehill in the middle and Totmonslow in the north. Colton is situated in Pirehill. The names may have originated from meeting place names established in the early Anglo Saxon period.

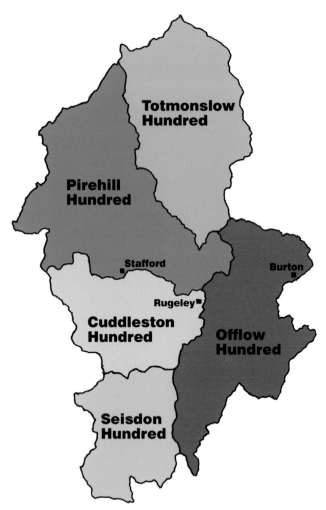

The Hundreds of Staffordshire

The New Norman landowners in Staffordshire

There emerged two types of landholders to replace the old Anglo Saxon ones. Nearly all the Staffordshire Anglo Saxon thegns were usurped and 11 Norman tenants in chief were given land by the King. The tenants in chief were the great Norman knights who had accompanied William at the Conquest and were rewarded by him for their support. He needed their support to help him stamp out any rebellion against his rule by the Anglo Saxons he had conquered. In the first few years following the Conquest, he had to work hard at asserting his authority in many parts of the country. These great lords were to provide him with the knights he needed in return for their land. They held land directly from the King and their Staffordshire holdings would only be one fraction of their overall land holdings scattered around many parts of the country. These holdings became known as 'honours' or 'manors'. Often a settlement would have its land divided between more than one manorial lord as was the case in Colton where there were two lords. One lord owned two manors, the other, one manor. In return for their land they had to provide services to the King in the form of a fixed quota of fully armed and equipped knights whenever he needed them.

The Church

William did not want interference from the Church in Rome regarding the religious houses and cathedrals in England and he therefore appointed his own bishops and abbots in place of the Saxon ones, bringing his appointees over from

Normandy. Leofwine, Bishop of Lichfield was made to resign. The Church however was allowed to keep its previous landholdings and also was given more land. Those religious establishments that had existed before the Conquest, such as Burton Abbey, the Cathedral at Lichfield and the Canons of Stafford and Wolverhampton, retained their lands and were given more. Staffordshire land holdings were also given to Westminster Abbey and the Church of St. Remy in Rheims, France. Steadily other abbeys and priories such as Tutbury were established and these too acquired land usually gifted to them by members of these Norman noble families. Burton Abbey acquired many new land holdings in this early period.

The tenants who worked on the land

The tenants in chief sub let their estates to their own followers and created a second group of under tenants holding land not directly from the king but from these Norman earls and lords. They in turn were being rewarded for their allegiance and they too had to provide military services.

The landholders of Saxon times who had been known as 'ceurls', now became the under tenants on the manors of these Norman lords and were referred to as "Villeins" "Bordars" and "Cottars" in the Domesday survey. In this great upheaval they lost many of the rights that they had had as ceurls. They now held their land and dwellings from the Norman lords as under tenants and were subject to his demands. They were required to give so many days service each week to the lord. This meant that the majority of the population of this country were now totally reliant upon their manorial lord and the whole system was beholden to one King rather than to regional kings as it had been until almost the end of the Anglo Saxon period.

What was included in the Domesday Survey

The Domesday Survey was ordered by William for the purpose of establishing who had held what possessions before his arrival and who held them in 1086. Also it was to give some indication as to the value of those possessions. Although the Survey did not cover the whole of the country, it is a remarkable statistical document for its time and was very thorough in recording what was in all the vills (manors) and towns. Staffordshire was one of the counties that were surveyed. "…not one ox, nor one cow nor one pig escaped notice in his survey".[1]

The Manors

The vills or manors were valued by the recorded number of inhabitants living there; the number of ploughs that were in use on the land in the manor; the amount of land; the amount of wood and any asset such as a mill.

The system of dividing the ploughland within the village to make it fair was based on each person having parcels of land usually in strips (a strip being a practical length of a piece of land a 'furlong' long - 210 metres long by 20 metres wide.) possibly the distance that a team of oxen could draw a plough without pausing to rest. The difficult job was turning the plough as they reached the end of the strip. Each strip eventually assumed the shape of an elongated S as they turned the ox team at the end. Even now if you look at an OS map of Colton you will see some fields around the village that still have boundaries shaped in this way. Each person's strips were spread around the manor so that the good and poorer land would be distributed evenly.

All the work on the manor was done in a communal way for practicality. The seasons dictated the tasks with everyone carrying out these various tasks such as ploughing sowing, reaping, hedging, ditching etc. at the same time and helping each other. This way the manor ran like one big farm although each family tenanted different sized units within the manor according to their status. The lord obviously had the most, followed by the villeins and then the cottars and bordars. Some villeins would have larger holdings than others. There were only villeins recorded in Colton. The only bit of land the slaves might have would be a small garden.

Pictures courtesy of Staffs County Council Ed. Dept.

Ploughing

Sowing seed

Harrowing

Harvesting

Threshing

The manor would be worked in a three field cycle, a practice that went back way before the Normans arrived. One field was ploughed and sown in Autumn with a corn crop such as wheat, one ploughed and sown in Spring with oats or barley or peas, and one left fallow with no crop so that the animals could graze on it and manure it. The field that was fallow this year would be Autumn sown next year and spring sown the year after. In this way the land did not become exhausted.

Colton and its inhabitants at the time of Domesday

Colton was held by the two great Norman lords– Earl Roger and Robert of Stafford. As King William's commissioner (the scribe who was sent out by royal command to record all the holdings) made his way towards the settlement of Colton to record the holdings of these two Norman overlords and to make his assessment for the Domesday entry, what was he likely to have seen and found?

On his way possibly from the direction of Stafford the nearest town, he may have walked through the great forest of Cannock. This central part of Staffordshire had huge forests. No one was allowed to hunt in the great oak forest of Cannock where deer, boar and other forest animals ran wild. This like the other forests in the land, was the preserve of the King and a few favoured companions. "The law of the forest was directed to the single end of protecting the wild beasts so that they might be found in abundance for the king's hunting" [2]. There was also a purpose behind this as well as 'royal pleasure'. In the years before the Conquest the cutting down of forest land and the making of "assarts" to bring more land into agricultural production had intensified and probably would have continued if William had not made many of these forests royal preserves. Wild animals such as deer would probably also have very soon become extinct. The Chief Forester appointed by the king to see over the forests and his officials, the 'verderers', generally four in each forest and chosen in the Shire Court, were distrusted and disliked. Poaching in these royal forests was a serious crime covered by a very strict "Forest Law". They had powers to arrest any poachers and punish them severely usually loss of limbs but also loss of life if you were caught re-offending. To those people who lived in small communities within the forest such as at "Aggardsley" in the Forest of Needwood, near Newborough, to be surrounded by the abundance of wildlife and not to be able to take any of it to provide for daily living, must have been very difficult. It was not until concessions were wrung from King John at the end of the Barons' War that some of these restrictions were relaxed and provided remedies for the long standing grievances concerning 'Forest Law'. The forests were the hiding place for outlaws as well as the realm of dangerous animals such as wolves and boar. To walk through them was a hazardous business.

When the scribe finally arrived on the outskirts of Colton he would have found a sizeable settlement; in fact probably the biggest settlement between Stafford and Lichfield. If he entered the village from the nearest town of Stafford, over the Moreton Brook, to his left where the modern day Boughey Hall buildings stand; he would have seen an area that appeared to be wasteland and marsh. It was not cultivated because it was prone to bogginess due to the high water table.

What the Norman settlement of Colton may have looked like

Moreton Brook was partly fed by a spring that ran down the route of the present day Bellamour Way. This has been the main route into and through the village for centuries and was probably the route he took then. He would be walking along a muddy pathway more than likely running with water according to weather conditions. This small tributary to the brook ran along the trackway until the late 18th. Century when it was finally culverted under the road. (Until the 20th. Century it was known as Brook Street.)

Before he entered the settlement he would have passed meadows down by the River Trent that regularly flooded in the winter, providing lush grass that would be cut for the nutrient rich hay to be fed to the cows in order to fatten them up before many of them were slaughtered in late Summer to

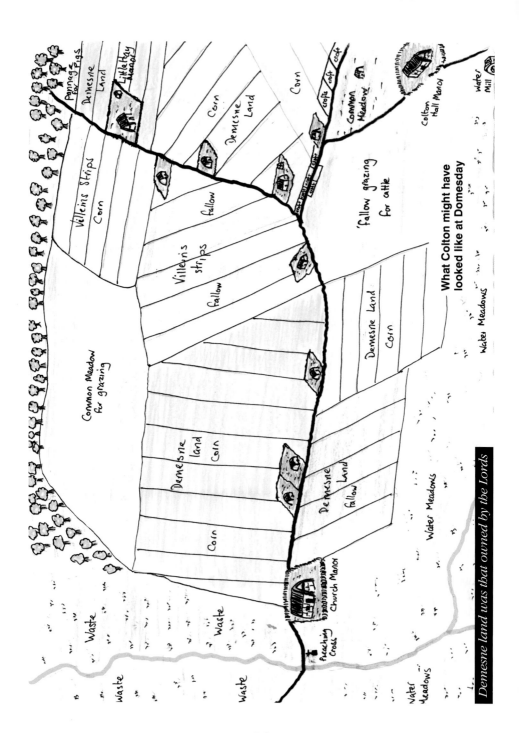

What Colton might have looked like at Domesday

Demesne land was that owned by the Lords

provide much needed food for the winter months. He would also have passed some of the fields worked in strips on the demesne land belonging to the lord of the manor and also some worked by the villeins of Colton. The only clues we now have as to where the strips might have been in Colton are from some field names, a little information in some deeds and a small amount of physical evidence. Many of the field names will go back to this period if not before. The evidence from deeds mentions strips in Hamley Fields, Parchfields, Trent Field and a field close to Colton water mill. Also there was a court case in 1351 [3] which referred to the tenants of a number of strips and how scattered they were. The visible surface evidence has now almost gone. Ridges and furrows made by the ploughs were visible until the late 20th. Century on land behind Little Hay Manor. We also know there were some behind the houses in High Street observable and recorded from aerial photographs after the Second World War but not visible at ground level.

As he crossed the stream he may have seen a church and a stone preaching cross stood close by. (There is the base of a preaching cross next to a side wall of the present church). This cross or church would have alerted him to the fact that this was one of only 33 settlements in Staffordshire where a priest lived.

We have no evidence of a church at Domesday although there is a strong possibility that there was one because of the size of the settlement. If there was, it would more than likely have been built of timber, wattle and daub not stone and would have been built close to the stream. The Saxons always sited their churches close to water.

This is the future site of a new stone church built sometime in the following century.

As he got closer to the dwellings that straddled the rough muddy track that ran through the settlement, he would be met by strong smells and the noise of animals. The smells would emanate from the human latrine pits next to the houses and the animal dung heaps that would also be close by ready to be used to fertilize the gardens and fields. Chickens, dogs and cats would all be rummaging in and around the houses. The pigs, an important source of food, would be in the woods and coppices that surround the village, snuffling in the undergrowth for pannage.

The houses would be small, wood, wattle and daub buildings with one room only. They would probably be supported by a timber frame called a crook frame. This was hewn out of single timbers and erected in an A shape to give the building strength.

When he met any of the residents they would be dressed in coarse woollen garments. The men would be wearing a knee length tunic with a belt and woollen leggings whereas the women would wear a full length hooded garment secured with a belt.

The world of the villein was the village and the field. These villagers would have risen at dawn ready to perform the tasks of cultivating the land; with some urgency if it is their own holding or probably with grumbling reluctance if the day is one set aside for work on the lord's land. They will be thinking of the programme of jobs that are to be done in the months ahead, hopefully with the co-operation of their neighbours; the obligations to the lord that have to be met and if they will be able to produce enough food to keep the family through the year.

BUILDING A VILLEIN'S HOUSE

THERE WAS NO CHIMNEY. SMOKE ROSE UP THROUGH A SMALL HOLE IN THE ROOF

IN THE MIDDLE OF THE FLOOR WAS THE FIRE

THE FLOOR WAS MADE OF HARD TRAMPLED EARTH COVERED WITH HAY OR REEDS

THE WALLS WERE MADE OF WATTLE - TWIGS WOVEN TOGETHER, AND PLASTERED WITH A MIXTURE OF MUD AND STRAW CALLED DAUB

If they are ploughing they will probably be met at lunch time by a member of the family who would bring them bread, cheese and a jug of ale. After the heavy work of ploughing the strip in the morning, they will return with the oxen to the village where they are turned out on the communal field.

At home younger children will have spent the day gathering firewood, searching for eggs, bird scaring, stone picking and searching for scraps of wool from the sheep to make clothes. Wives may have been weaving to provide them with clothes.

The evening will be around a communal hearth in the centre of their simple one roomed dwelling where a stew type meal mainly of vegetables, meat if they were lucky to have some left or perhaps rabbit. The Normans had introduced rabbits to this country and they were soon providing a rich source of food for people throughout the year, often when there was very little else to eat. Bread would be made from flour that they would have had to pay the lord to have milled at the water mill down by the crossing on the Trent. This mill belonged to the lord that lived on the eastern side of the settlement. Soon they would retire to bed because there was no longer light to see by.

The Manor near the church

This would have been the first substantial dwelling of some size he would have seen on the right hand side. This was larger than the other dwellings because it belonged to the lord of the manor. This is the manor that would eventually carry the name of **'Church Manor'**.

This house is thought to have been sited over the brook just west of where the church eventually gets built on a piece of land that carried the name "Castle Croft".

As the scribe came closer, he would see that although this dwelling is bigger, as with all other houses in this part of the country, the walls would be made of wood, wattle and daub with a deep thatched roof and shutters at the window openings. Stone was not in use around this part of Staffordshire.

The scribe would have entered via a doorway into a large smoky house space with a big open hearth in the centre of

A Norman Manor

the space where some cooking was probably being done by house servants. At one end and probably on a slightly raised platform there would be rushes on the floor of the living space, a long table and benches. This raised area is where the new Norman lord and his family would be living, dining and sleeping when they were in residence in Colton and not visiting one of their other manors. At this time there would be no private spaces or bedrooms. The only other furniture in the house would probably be a couple more benches and a couple of chests as furniture and possibly some cloth hangings by the window openings ready to cover the windows to keep out the draughts and the cold. There would be no glass in the windows.

The Norman lord and his wife would be better dressed than the other village occupants. Their clothes would be of a finer quality and would probably be made of wool imported from France. They would be speaking French as opposed to vernacular English of the locals. Speaking in French did not survive long into the Middle Ages, eventually only being spoken in the Royal court. The English language became the one great survivor of the time before the Norman Conquest.

Norman Lord and Lady

Along with the cooking smells he might be able to smell beeswax from the candles that were used last night to light this lord's house. The bees wax was an expensive and treasured item. The hives would be carefully tended somewhere in the village. The smell of cooking could indicate a piece of beef or some pork being cooked by one of the lord's slaves. The lord would live comparatively well compared to the rest of the inhabitants of Colton. However in the late winter months, food would be short in everybody's house, even the lord's, and starvation would be an ever present threat.

In this big house the scribe would meet the Norman lord Ascelin who held this manor as an under tenant from his master, the great Norman lord, Earl Roger. Roger had been foremost in King William's invading army and had been justly rewarded. This was one of the three manors the scribe was to record that day in Colton, sometime in 1086.

This is the first entry he made under the Colton holdings of Earl Roger.

"Colton. Ascelin holds from him. 1 hide. Land for 4 ploughs. Almund held it; he was free. In lordship 2 ploughs; 4 slaves. 14 villeins with a priest have 3 ploughs.

Meadow 19 acres; woodland 1 league long and ½ wide.

Value 40s". (Ref 8:15 Domesday)

We know Earl Roger was a great Norman soldier who had supported William by providing 60 ships for the invasion. He

38

had remained in Normandy and ensured its safety whilst William was in England [4]. He came to England in 1067. In 1071 he was created Earl of Shrewsbury and was the chief lord of the Welsh Marches. He eventually fell out of favour with William when he led a rebellion of men from Wales, Cheshire and Staffordshire. Some of his forces were defeated by William at Stafford. He died in 1094. Roger's son, Robert, later rebelled against the King and lost all of their lands when they were confiscated by Henry I.

We know little of Ascelin other than he held 3 other manors in Pirehill Hundred, Cote, Ridware and Loxley besides Colton. Frederick Parker in his book about Colton [4] suggests that he was given these manors because he held castle guard for Earl Roger in the Welsh Marches but he cites no evidence for this.

Almund was the Saxon who had held the land previously and who had been usurped by Earl Roger.

Ascelin's holding of 1 hide would be roughly 120 acres. Part of this would be the ploughable arable land which was worked by his 4 slaves using his 2 ploughs. They would be assisted by the 14 villeins and the priest on the days they were obliged to work for him, probably using their ploughs as well because the area was large enough to require 4 ploughs to work it. The villeins as tenants of Ascelin would work their holdings he had granted them using their three ploughs that they probably owned communally. There was a high number of ploughs on this manor so they possibly hired them out to the adjacent manors that had fewer ploughs.

The 19 acres of meadow would again have been looked after by everybody.

The woodland was approximately 1 and a ½ miles long and ¾ of a mile wide. It was a substantial amount of woodland and was probably split up into smaller woods around the village. The villeins would have to pay for the privilege of letting their pigs run with their lord's pigs in these woods eating the pannage to fatten them up. They would also be the source of the timber to build their houses and fuel for their fires which again they would have to pay the lord for.

Having recorded this manor the scribe carried on through the settlement. He would be passing smaller wattle and daub houses that lay on either side of the track and belonged to the villeins who lived on this manor. As to where precisely all these houses were we have no evidence as such. However village plans have evolved over centuries and as Colton follows a linear pattern working its way along from the Church, past the Church Manor house based by the church, up the hill towards Little Hay Manor; it is more than likely that some of the villeins' houses belonging to this manor were scattered along this route.

Little Hay Manor

He was on his way to a second smaller manor tenanted by Ascelin. The house for this manor was sited on the right hand side of the track that we now know as High Street. Later it became the manor known as **Little Hay**.

There he recorded a second entry for the Domesday Book but this time under the name COLT.

"In Colt there is ½ hide which belongs to Colton. Aelmar held it". (Ref. 8:16)

Again it is listed in the holdings of Earl Roger. The under tenant is not named but as it is the next holding listed we can fairly safely assume that this was also held by Ascelin from Earl Roger. Aelmar was the Saxon who had been usurped. This is a smaller manor with approximately 60 acres and probably would have been worked by the same villeins who worked the Church manor as they are not enumerated separately in this entry.

The scribe would then move on along a track over the Martlin Hill (we do not know when it became known as this) to record the third manor in this settlement of Colton. This manor lay a little distance away from the main area of settlement over to the east in the direction of Hill Ridware and was accessed by a path from Bank Top.

Colton Hall Manor

Here he recorded his entry under the holdings of Robert of Stafford.

"In Colton 1 hide. Geoffrey holds from him. Oda and Wulfric held it; they were free. Land for 6 ploughs. In lordship 1; 10 villeins and 1 slave with 3 ploughs.

A mill at 12d; meadow 16 acres woodland 1 league long and 3 furlongs wide.

Value 50s". (Ref 11:29)

Geoffrey was under tenant to Sir Robert. We do know something of Geoffrey. He appears to have been from a Norman family known as de Gastiney from Normandy. He was a follower of Sir Robert and was granted lands by him in Lincolnshire at Osgarthorp and also at Colton in

Staffordshire.[4] The name in the early 12th Century changed to de Wasteneys and as such the de Wasteneys family owned the manor in Colton until well into the 14th Century. This manor became known as **Colton Hall Manor**.

Geoffrey like Ascelin held 1 hide that is 120 acres. Oda and Wulfric had been the two Saxons who had been usurped. There was 1 plough owned by Geoffrey. There appears to have been a large area of his holding under cultivation because it required 6 ploughs to work it. The 10 villeins on this manor owned 3 ploughs and so they probably used their ploughs also to work his arable strips as well as their own strips. 16 acres of his land are used as meadow. The wood measured 1½ miles by 3 furlongs and although it would have belonged to Geoffrey, like the wood on the other Colton manor it would be used by the villeins on this manor. The lord would have the timber rights for the better timber that would be used for building, usually oak in this part of Staffordshire. We think remainders of these woods are still there today and known as Hurst Wood and Old Wood. They were certainly on the land we know that belonged to this manor.

The water mill on the Trent was the great asset to this manor and would bring in a considerable income. Sited on the Trent this water mill would be used for grinding corn. It would more than likely also be used by other surrounding manors. There would also be eel and fish traps by the water mill on this part of the Trent again a prized possession. In later centuries there are records of disputes concerning fishing rights on this stretch of the river.

Estimate of the population of Colton in 1086

The scribe recorded the total value of the three manors of Colton as 90 shillings; the Church manor as 40 shillings and Colton Hall manor as 50 shillings. This value was greater than any of the other settlements in the immediate vicinity. It also had a larger population. Working on the principle of 5 people per family unit it had –

Church Manor

4 slaves = 20 souls
14 villeins = 70 souls
1 priest = 5 souls

Colton Hall Manor

1 slave = 5 souls
10 villeins = 50 souls

150 altogether.

This number would increase each time the respective lords of the two manors were in residence with their entourages and not at one of their other estates.

This made Colton the largest settlement in the vicinity, much larger than Rugeley that eventually overtook it in size. It must have been a place of some significance for the times. Was this why it had a Priest?

The Church Manor land appears to have been based around the church and running south and west of the village over towards Admaston following the Rugeley/Admaston road. Little Hay Manor land we think was based north and west of the village on the hill behind the present day farm house, whilst Colton Hall Manor was south and east of the village and included the Martlin Hill, land down to the Trent and also over towards the Newlands.

As the scribe walked out of the village of Colton on his way to the next settlement, he left behind him a village that was already well established and would continue to thrive with few changes for many years to come.

Notes

1. Anglo Saxon Chronicles New Addition Michael Swanton Phoenix Press.

2. English Society in the Early Middle Ages Doris May Stenton Pelican History of England 3 1991.

3. Staffs. Historical Collection 1 Staffs. Record Office.

4. Rev. P. Parker Colton and the de Wasteneys. Private Publ. 1879 Staffs Record Office.

Chapter Four

Colton in the
Medieval Period

Colton in the Medieval Period

As the country settled down and accepted their new Norman manorial overlords, a system of organisation began to emerge in the villages which became known as 'the Parish'. There had been some organisation before in the settlements in Saxon times but not to the extent that it now began to develop.

As the Parish system evolved there were three focal points to the structure: the manors within the village, the church and lastly but by no means least, the community. As already noted in the previous chapter, the lords of the manors had a great amount of power in the community as their tenants were totally beholden to them for their land and little could happen without their permission. The lands belonging to these manors soon established the Parish boundaries. The manor court, presided over by the lord of the manor, was also the main centre for local village organisation and for justice. Here the local lord dictated everything that happened on his manor, until around the late 13th century when the day to day running of the village began to shift more to the community. For example from the mid 13th century onwards a constable was often elected from the village to take on the responsibility for maintenance of law and order within the parish.

When the Normans came they brought strong Christian religious beliefs with them and a desire to demonstrate this by building churches, abbeys, cathedrals and priories as they had done in France. All over the country they soon embarked on buildings of this nature. Soon the local preaching crosses of the Saxon period that had been used by travelling priests for outside services and the few Saxon churches more often made of wood, were replaced by stone churches built by local lords.

The local lord would take on the responsibility of erecting a church upon the manor for himself, his family and the inhabitants of the village to worship in on a regular basis. In Colton's case the church was erected by the lord of the Church Manor. The priest was appointed by the manorial lord and was maintained in the church at the expense of the community by tithes i.e. payments of goods and produce both large and small. Everyone on the manor was obliged to contribute one tenth of their produce to pay the lord for his church and to maintain the priest in his office. The large tithes were such things as sheep and cows, hay, corn; the smaller ones were such as ducks, apples and eggs. This practice existed well into the early part of the twentieth century except by then most of the tithes had been converted into money payments.

Unlike today, religion played a huge part in every one's day to day life. Religious beliefs and practices heavily influenced how people conducted their lives from the highest in society to the lowliest village dweller. The church led the way in setting the everyday Christian religious observances which became the nucleus around which the pattern of life was conducted and parochial organisation developed. Religion provided a yearly framework of special religious occasions closely tied in with the pattern of the working year throughout the seasons.

Payment of tithes to the Manorial Lord.

As already stated the 13th Century onwards saw the village community taking on more and more responsibility for local matters, especially such matters as maintaining the fabric of the church, maintaining the religious rights that were practised within the church and other responsibilities that affected the village. This was all done through a parish organisation that soon became known as the 'Vestry', called by this name because the meetings were originally held in the Vestry of the Church, probably because there was no where else to meet. At a later date many villages built a church house where lots of activities would take place. These Vestry meetings became the natural successor to the manor court except for administering justice which stayed with the manor court. Colton's two manor courts were held at Colton Hall and Little Hay Manor. The last record we have of the Colton Hall Manor Court is in the late 17th Century but Little Hay Manor Court still functioned until the late 19th century.

People waiting for judgement at the Manorial Court

The Vestry comprised elected individuals from the village who had oversight of both matters pertaining to the church and the parish and the responsibility of generating the income to maintain these institutions and providing village inhabitants to take responsibility for them. The principal office within the vestry was that of church warden. It was a very onerous and responsible position and there was always a great obligation to make sure that the church and the parish was well run and that they complied with the demands put upon them. Over the centuries and particularly in the Tudor period more and more responsibilities were laid upon these parish officers by the state and greater demands were made of them. They became responsible for organising such things as collection of local taxes, providing local militias, maintenance of the highways, local law and order between the parishes and looking after the poor of the parish.

Vestry minute books survive for Colton from the 17th Century onwards and give an insight into the workings of this body in Colton.

It is against this backdrop that we can now take a look at life in Colton during this period.

Life and Events in Colton. 1086-1485

The general everyday work life of the villagers would not have changed much in this period. Life was exceptionally hard and almost totally tied to the soil. The village would have had its smith and other tradesmen to support the work on the land.

The Normans had not invented the bonds of feudalism but they extended it. The people of the village had to exchange protection for services in a way that was far more onerous than had ever been before. It meant that most of the fruits of their labours were going into the pockets of their Norman landlords. The Norman overlords were prevented by law from killing or maiming their tenants yet they could be sold along with estates with great ease like selling a horse, a field or some timber and exactly this happened in Colton. The population surprisingly began to grow dramatically throughout the 12th century into the early 13th Century. This put a lot of pressure on the cultivation of land and more and more assarts (pieces of land) were cut out of the woodlands. This also happened in Colton when the area which became known as the Newlands was brought into cultivation. There are many mentions of this area of Colton in documents and it seems also that there were more dwellings there in this early period than later on. There is also an area in Colton Parish known as the "Hilliards" and this word means enclosures. It also appears that a water mill was built on the Blythe in this period and that at one point the miller was "Thomas of the Newlands" although it appears to have been owned by the Abbot of Burton.[1]

In 1348 the Black Death hit this country and wiped out between a third and a half of the population. We have found no records to date that it affected Colton. There does not appear to have been a decline in population. On the contrary Colton appears to be thriving possibly taking advantage of the effects the Black Death was causing elsewhere.

The Ownership of the Manors

The Church Manor and Little Hay Manor

The first change of ownership on the manors in Colton after the recording of the settlement for the Domesday record was a change in the over lordship of the Church Manor and Little Hay Manor.

In 1100 Henry I (third son of William the Conqueror) succeeded to the throne. His brother Robert disputed his claim and forced a rebellion by some of the powerful Norman earls including Earl Roger of Montgomery's son, Robert de Belleme, overlord of two of the Colton manors. This rebellion was eventually put down by the king in 1106 and the Montgomerys' had their lands confiscated, including the land in Colton.

Records from this period show that these two manors passed to a new overlord, the Fitz Alans', sometime between 1135 and 1160 from the Montgomery's.[2] The Fitz Alans' appear to have let fairly quickly to a Walter Hussey or Hose. At the time of the Domesday record Ascelin had been the sub tenant on these two Colton manors but by 1135 he had died and the tenancy had passed to his heirs the Mavesyn family. The Mavesyn's now become tenants of Walter Hose or Hussey who held the manors in Colton from the Fitz Alans'.[3]

The Mavesyn family were descendents of Ascelin and Hugh Mavesyn, the third in descent from Ascelin, established a house on a hill in the district of Blithbury. Whilst there, somewhere between 1130 and 1149, he established St. Giles's Priory for nuns near the River Blythe where the present day Priory Farm stands. Sometime soon after he moved his house to what we now know as the village of Mavesyn Ridware.[4] His heirs at a later date built a larger manor house there with a gatehouse and the gatehouse is still standing today. There is a tomb to Sir Hugh in Mavesyn Ridware church.

There appears to have been two branches of the Mavesyn family, the main line coming from Hugh. It is possibly this elder line of the family who were the tenants at the Church manor and the other younger branch of the family occupied the Little Hay Manor.[5] Assize records place Nicholas Mavesyn at Little Hay in 1203 when he is recorded as 'being at issue with some of his neighbours'. It would appear that fairly early on the elder line of Mavesyns' disappeared from the sub tenancy of the Church Manor and two new sub tenants the Griffyns and the De Coltons' take it over but the younger line remain sub tenants at Little Hay Manor.

Sometime at the beginning of the 13th century the overlordship of these two manors – the Church Manor and little Hay Manor again changes.[6] They pass from the Fitz Alans' and now become the property of William De Mareschal. The earliest evidence for this is that John Maraschal (grandson of William De Maraschal) received a pardon from Henry 111 for his father's part in the Baron's rebellion against the king. Records show that he did homage for the return of the family estates including the Colton Manors in 1249.[7]

As already mentioned, during this period Little Hay manor is still sub-tenanted by the Mavesyns' whilst the Church Manor appears for many years to have been tenanted by two families; the Griffins and the De Colton's.

The De Colton's appear at the Church Manor in a Pipe Roll record (a manor court record) of 1176[8] where Thomas De Colton is fined two marcs for forest trespass. However Alice De Colton marries William Griffyn in 1203 and they appear to amalgamate the families. The De Colton's disappear around the 1350's from the records of this manor and the Griffyns around 1396.

Who built Colton Church?

Priests were presented (appointed) to Colton church according to the records (see Church record in appendix.) from 1086 the time of Domesday. We know there was a priest in Colton prior to the conquest and there could well have been an earlier church erected in the Saxon period that continued to operate until the new church was built.

It is probably the Mareschal family who built Colton Church

when they became overlords of the Church Manor but we have no evidence to support this.

The building that stands today shows evidence of part of the tower being built possibly in the very late Norman period (13th Century). Various walls, windows and doorways date from the Early English period of architecture, the style that emerged in the 13th Century in this country. The change from Norman to Early English was progressive and would not have happened all at once all over the country. Village churches such as Colton would not have been in the vanguard of the changing architectural styles that were occurring at cathedrals and abbeys. This Early English style of architecture would fit in with the period of the over lordship of the Mareschals' which starts in the 13th Century. A deed dated 1277[9] and again one in 1282[10] state that William le Mareschal had the advowson of the Church of St. Mary and that it is worth 20 marks. This shows that he owns the church by then. Could this be evidence that it has been completed by then? Lady Avice le Mareschal presents a Priest in 1303.

The last mention of the Mareschal family in connection with the Colton Church Manor is in 1360 at the death of Anselm de Mareschal but by then the manor has passed by descent to the Morley Family. The Morleys' present a priest to the church in Colton in 1338.

What did the church in Colton look like?

External

This early church in Colton would probably have been quite small. From the physical evidence we have remaining it would probably have consisted of a tower, a nave, (present day nave and south aisle) a chapel possibly a chantry chapel (present day vestry) a chancel (present day chancel) and a porch. The Early English wall remaining on the south side still contains a small opening with a wooden door. This was probably used before the Reformation by any person with an infectious disease, such as leprosy who was not allowed inside the church, to view the Priest raising the "host" at the celebration of Mass.

Colton Church Plan Late 12th Century Early 13th Century

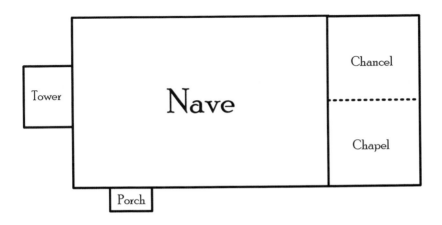

Colton Church Plan Possibly 13th Century Early 14th Century

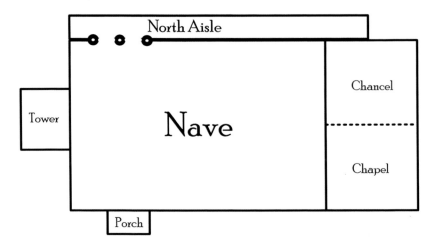

*Some little time later a north aisle was added
but we do not know when.*

To the lord of the manor the erection of a church would
have been an important display of wealth and piety. This was
an age when Christians had a strong belief in the Last Day
of Judgement. Purgatory was where your soul resided until
judgement and the main thrust of religious teaching was
that your behaviour in this life determined how long you
stayed in purgatory before judgement. The Priest was the
intercessor between you and God. He could pray on your
behalf to ease your passage through purgatory and good
works such as the erection of churches and chapels would
help in this intercession. This belief led to a proliferation
of donations by many to cathedrals, abbeys, churches and
chapels and some of the grandest ecclesiastical buildings
were built in this country during the period on the back of
this belief.

The Church as it looks today having had a Victorian restoration in 1851 which destroyed many of its earlier features. However, the architect, Street, did preserve some features.

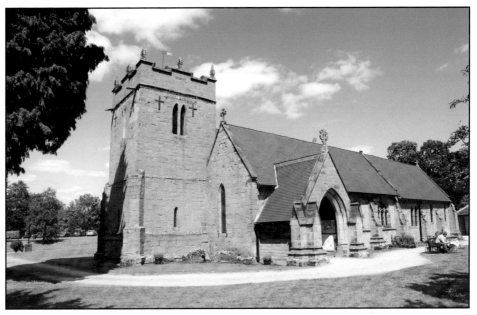

Possibly original chapel with
Early english windows and doorway.

The Tower with Early English windows.

Base of early medieval pillar.

The Leper's window or Squint.

Sedilia and Piscenae preserved in what is now the vestry but was a side Chapel

The new church in Colton would soon have been at the heart of village life and activities. In an English church of this period it was a place where not only religious ceremonies were held but also where most of the village business was conducted. In the beginning the nave was the meeting place for the villagers and on many occasions it would probably have been a noisy, busy place where the regular celebrations of the church year took place alongside the business of the parish.

The Chancel was the sacred area and the part of the church that was reserved for the priest. There the celebration of mass took place almost in secrecy behind a wooden screen known as a rood screen. This screen that in bigger churches would have statues of Christ, the Virgin Mary and St. John mounted on top, divided the religious liturgies from the general populace and they were only allowed to observe them by peeping through the screen. It all added to the atmosphere of mystery that the church encouraged in order to hold the congregation in awe. The Rood screens were one of the first things that Henry VIII had torn down in the Reformation.

Religious Celebrations

In all English churches there soon emerged a series of special days that linked the church to the passage of the seasons and the round of daily life. There were a number of major religious celebrations throughout the year and they had to be paid for and supported by the parish. Many involved candles which were a very expensive item. The purchase of candles for lighting the church and for lighting when Masses were said for the souls of the dead, became a big item in the expenditure of the church by the village and there emerged a number of ways in which the parish would collect money for them. The main way of raising money in most parishes became the brewing and selling of church ale. In a time when water was almost undrinkable because of the lack of hygiene, ale was the main drink, especially on festive days.

The religious year soon settled into a similar pattern of special days, celebrated and enjoyed by the entire village.

For instance Colton's annual Wake was celebrated on the 8th September. It celebrated the feast of Nativity of the Blessed Virgin Mary. This is the date when there would be a visiting fair in Colton and there would be much fun and festivity.

Although not all of these days were celebrated in every village around the country, Colton would have celebrated most of them. Rev. Parker in his book on Colton refers to the fact that even in his time (late 19th Century) there was an ancient custom of going "souling"on the evening of All Saints' Day. Also that the children went "Hallowing", going back to when money was raised to pay for candles to say masses for the dead. Another custom that lived on until the 19th Century was to help celebrate the Feast of the Nativity and it was performed by the women of the village. On that day they would collect a jug of corn and take it to be ground at the mill on the Trent. They would then add the ground corn to a beef broth also containing fruit called a "Frumity", in order to thicken it. It was then served to the poor and old of the village. This custom finished in 1880 when the water mill ceased to grind corn and became a plaster mill. Many of the other celebrations mentioned such as Plough Sunday and the May Day celebrations existed well into the late 20th Century. *(Plough Sunday has been recently celebrated by the Colton Church congregation).*

*May Day celebrations in the 19th
and 20th centuries in Colton*

As time went on the Colton Church, like all the parish churches around the country, became more and more elaborate inside. There would probably have been lots of small niches around the side chapel wall dedicated to different saints where candles would be burning at certain times. There would have been wall paintings all around the building as will be mentioned further on in this chapter and possibly at least one more altar in the side chapel, decorated as would be the main alter in the Chantry with crosses and plates. This plate would be constantly being added to and paid for by the Parish.

As it was now a sizeable village with a regular weekly market and therefore a local centre for the area, Colton would have regular fairs visiting on various occasions

Colton Hall Manor

We know nothing of Colton Hall Manor until about 80 years after the Domesday entry but it would appear that it stayed with the heirs of Geoffrey de Gastineys (Domesday entry) and sometime in this period the name changes to 'de Wasteneys'. The first record we have of the change of name relating to their Colton Manor comes in a deed from the Ridware Deeds dated 1158, where Geoffrey (a descendant of the first Geoffrey) signs the deed 'de Wasteneys' along with members of the Bagot family. Also there is a signature of his heir, Sir Philip, in 1200 on a charter of the Bishop of Lichfield's concerning land at the Lount estate in Colton of which there will be more later.

The end of the 12th century and the beginning of the 13th century were again turbulent times in this country with a period of great unrest in the reign of King John (1199-1216).

Many of the lords rebelled against his rule which eventually culminated in him being forced to sign Magna Carta.

From records that have survived[11] we know that Sir Philip de Wasteneys was opposed to King John although he did eventually do homage to him by providing military service. He had apparently been captured at Mount Sorrel in Leicestershire whilst fighting against the king's forces. He was taken as a prisoner to Nottingham where John le Mareschal (overlord of the church and Little Hay Manors), and a strong supporter of King John, illegally forced the surrender of Sir Philip's land including Colton Hall Manor; to him. This enforced surrender was probably what opened Sir Philip's prison door. When Sir Philip eventually showed allegiance to the King, he was told that his lands would be returned to him.[12] However he then had to sue "le Mareschal" of Colton to get his manor back.[13] Sir Philip died somewhere between 1228 and 1235.

By 1240 the de Wasteneys appear to become a lot more interested and actively involved in the affairs of their Colton Manor probably because they see it as an opportunity to make money. This is the period when a lot of sizeable villages are granted Market Charters and in 1240 Sir Philip's son and heir, Sir William de Wasteneys, is granted the right to hold a weekly market in Colton by King Henry III. This reflects the size and importance of Colton at that time because it receives its Market Charter some years before Rugeley, the place that eventually overshadows Colton. The market charter gives permission for a market to be held every Friday. It seems strange now to think of Colton being big enough to have its own market!

They also now appear to have two other mills on the Manor. Besides the money making water mill on the Trent recorded in Domsday, they also erect a mill at Hamley.

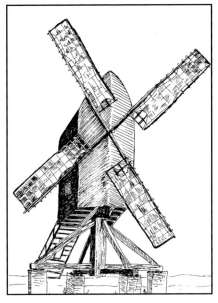

This mill is mentioned in a lawsuit brought in Edward I's time. Although it is not known exactly where it was sited, field names in the village such as "mill ditch" and "part of mill ditch" give us some clues. There is also a field nearby called "Wilmer". This name has turned up in records for centuries and is possibly a corruption of the word "windmill"[14]. Therefore it is quite probable that the site of this was where the windmill stood or nearby. There is also a strong possibility that there was a third mill at Hamley alluded to in a deed.[15] This could possibly have been another water mill because the Muln Brook runs close by and could have powered this mill.

The fourth Sir William de Wasteneys, who succeeded to the Colton lands about 1240, also took a great interest in his Colton Manor. In 1257 he is recorded as giving 11½ acres of his land to St Thomas's priory in Stafford.[16] This again is an example of the practice by the wealthy of giving gifts to priories and abbeys in this period. The Augustinian Priory of St. Thomas the Martyr had been established in 1174 on the

River Sow in Stafford by such gifts and continued to receive many more gifts until by the Dissolution it was one of the richest priories in Staffordshire.

Locally some land at the "Lount" on the edges of Colton Parish had already been given by its owner to the priory. The Priory established a Grange farm on this land with the tithes and probably a lot of the produce going directly to the Priory. The rest of the land known as the Lount would eventually pass into the hands of the Gresley family in the next century.

The Colton piece of land was part of the land that was probably fairly boggy. It is recorded in Domseday lying to the left of Moreton Brook Bridge, as being "waste" *(see map of Colton Manor in previous chapter)*. It introduced another landowner into Colton and also became the site of a Grange farm for the Priory until it was eventually given away by Henry VIII at the dissolution of the monasteries and became known subsequently as Boughey Hall Farm.

Sir William also makes improvements to his manor. Like many men of his station at the time he is fond of hunting and the "chase". We know that he held the important role of "Justice of the Forest" helping to protect the great royal forest of Cannock for the king's sport of hunting. As the forests were the preserves solely of the King for this activity, the crown began to grant the "Right of free Warren" to manorial lords to create their own hunting grounds. It meant that they could enclose parts of their own manor to encourage various animals such as deer, foxes, hares, cats, badgers, squirrels and even the occasional wolf to thrive for hunting purposes. Henry III granted Sir William this right in 1264. He proceeded to create an enclosed park on his Colton Manor called

"The Old Park" for this purpose. The boundary remains of this park can still be seen in a field on the road from Colton to the Newlands today although it has now almost disappeared.

Old Park Boundary

We have some idea of the amount of game in this park from a court case[17] when a number of village residents are charged with park breaking and the stealing of game and are taken to court by the de Wasteneys. They are accused of taking 40 bucks, 100 does, 20 hares, 40 rabbits, 40 pheasants and a 1,000 partridges. Whether it was all at one go or over a period we have no idea.

This right was also granted to St Thomas's Priory on their Colton land by King Edward I in 1293.[18]

We have a remarkable insight into the management of the Colton Hall manor from some accounts that have survived from 1362-1363 in the time of Thomasine de Wasteneys. They had fortunately been preserved over the centuries amongst "Ingestre Deeds".

Here we have rents recorded on the manor, names of tenants, prices for sale of stock and crops e.g. "16s. received from the sale of 2 bulls, and 5s.6d for a swan".

Payments for work done such as sowing, threshing, feeding the horses and the swans. (The de Wasteneys appear to have had an "eerie" for swans on the Trent by the water mill.) Also "foreign expenses" such as 'fencing around the park'.

The accounts even record gloves that are given to "my lady".[19]

In the Colton records there are also Subsidy Rolls for the years 1327 and 1333.[20] The Subsidy Roll of 1327 contains 27 persons contributing whereas the one of 1333 contains only 16 names. It could be that the earlier one has the names of the occupants of all three manors and as Anselm Mareschal heads the list of the later one, these may only be the names of the Church and Little Hay Manor tenants. If this is so then in the first list of 1327 we remarkably have the names of the de Wasteneys Manor tenants at this date. Henry de Caldwell, John Clechok, William Maynard, John Galweye, William de Hondsacre, Reginald de Wasteneys, Adam Brown, Henry de Morhay, John Andreu, John le Counter, Xtiana Pourcey, Ralph Grym and Richard de Holihurst.

A Period of Lawlessness

Towards the end of the reign of Henry III there was considerable dissatisfaction with his rule. A revolt by Simon de Montfort caused great unrest and lawlessness. Although Simon de Montfort was killed in 1265 the lawlessness continued well into the reign of Edward I. This lack of law and order appears to have prevailed throughout the country and Colton did not escape.

The first evidence we have of this lawlessness in the Colton records is a murder around 1270. Nicholas son of William of Colton, stabbed Adam, son of Hereward in a brawl at Dutton. The murderer fled for sanctuary to Colton Church.

He was entitled to claim sanctuary in a church from the first hour of the day until midnight. The Colton villagers appear to have tried to secure his arrest by keeping him in the church. This was thwarted however by one Ralph de Burgh, who appears to have been prompted by William the Younger of the Maveyson family of Little Hay Manor, to help Nicholas escape. At an inquest into the death of Adam, the parishioners of Colton did not attend and were find 100 shillings by the Sheriff.[21]

Taking sanctuary

The following year 1271 there was a second murder, this time in Colton. "John, the chaplain of Colton, killed Christina, wife of Nicholas de Colton whilst interposing between him and a stranger residing at her house, striking her in the stomach with a knife, although the blow was really intended for her guest". John fled from justice and was outlawed, his goods being confiscated.[22] Judgement of murder in this case was given against the "Hundred" rather than the village and a fine of 66 marks were enforced.

A further murder took place outside Colton Hall Manor in the early 14th Century when Thomas of Colton quarrelled with William the son of the smith of Colton. Thomas struck William with a knife on the head and killed him. He fled and was immediately outlawed.[23] There were apparently 3 more murders committed in the village between 1270 and 1306.[24] Henry at Asch killed Adam, grandson of Walter de Colton; Ralph Griffyn and his brother murdered William le Contour and William Fox killed John Bonel. The de Coltons' and the Griffyns' seem to have been involved in many misdeeds within the village!

There are also records of robberies and of many disputes over parcels of land around the village throughout the 14th Century. Many of the early land disputes appear to be brought again by the Griffyn family, sub tenants of the Church Manor who seem to have been constantly arguing with their neighbours. There are numerous court records of these quarrels.

One particular dispute in 1250 over the pulling down of a hedge ends up with the Sheriff of Stafford coming to look at it. It is commonly believed that this visit by the Sheriff gave rise to the name of "Sherra Cop Lane" and was probably the lane on the disputed boundary.

In 1326 the valuable fishing rights on the Trent at Colton Mill are the cause of a vicious assault committed by the "people of Colton" including William Griffyn and others. They had come with swords, bows and arrows, beat the servants of Adam of Rugeley and stole the fishing nets.[25]

In the 1350's another court case over land this time involving Sir Thomas de Wasteneys, ended in violence. Sir Thomas charged William the smith and two others of coming with "swords, bows and arrows and taking marl, clay and sand from his several soil in Colton to the value of 100 shillings". He claimed £10 in damages. Could the marl have been from the large marl hole in Hollow Lane which we know was used for centuries by the village and possibly was the derivation for the name Martlin Hill?[26]

These are only a few of the many court cases that were brought in this period.

The de Wasteneys become the major landholders in Colton as the Manors again change hands.

In the second half of the 14th Century the de Wasteneys family seized the opportunity to become the major landholders in Colton.

Sir Thomas de Wasteneys died in 1350 leaving a wife, Joan Tolley and 4 heirs, William, John, Thomas and a daughter Thomasine. At his death Colton Hall Manor became the property for life of his wife Joan who in 1352 married a second husband, Sir John de Gresley. This link between the two families became greater when Thomasine married Sir John's son Nicholas, possibly around 1364.[27]

In 1363 Sir Thomas Morley, heir to the Le Mareschal manors in Colton, granted Sir John Gresley and Joan Tolley his wife, the Colton Church Manor rights in perpetuity. This meant that the Gresleys' now held the Church Manor, Colton Hall Manor, the advowsen to the church, the water mill on the Trent and the other two mills.[28]

With the introduction of the Gresley family this marks a major turning point in the history of Colton.

As an ancestor of Robert of Stafford (Domesday Record), Sir John Gresley, like the de Wasteneys, held land in Staffordshire and Derbyshire. His manor at Moreton bordered on the Parish of Colton. By acquiring the Church Manor he and his wife Joan consolidated into one the Moreton and Colton properties, with the exception of Little Hay and the Grange belonging to St. Thomas's Priory.

Thomasine succeeded to the whole of the Colton Estates when her three elder brothers died leaving her sole heir. By her marriage to Nicholas Gresley all her lands passed into the hands of the Gresley family and are inherited upon their deaths by their son Thomas de Gresley making him now the lord of the two main Manors in Colton. The family was now of some considerable wealth and standing demonstrated by the fact that his daughter became the nurse to King Henry VI.

At the restoration of Colton Church in the mid 19th century wall paintings were uncovered from beneath the whitewash on the walls of the present day vestry. This was probably a side chapel possibly a chantry chapel in the period of the de Wasteneys and it is thought that these paintings were done in the time of  Thomasine. The wall paintings of pictures depicting events from the bible and Saints were a common practice in all churches before the Reformation to help give instruction to the laity. As one of the pictures that was uncovered was dedicated to St. Nicholas, it has been suggested that possibly

Thomasine had had them painted in dedication to her husband Sir Nicholas Gresley, although we have no evidence.

Change of Ownership of Little Hay Manor

Little Hay also changes ownership in this period again by marriage. In 1322 a Blithfield deed shows that Robert the "Younger Lord of Littlehay" sold the Little Hay Manor to Richard de Blithfield but kept a life long interest in the property and continues to live there. Elizabeth the daughter and sole heiress of Richard de Blithfield married Sir Ralph Bagot of Bagots Bromley in 1361 and carried the Little Hay Manor into the hands of the Bagot family. They continued to own it until the mid 20th Century.

Thus by the time the Tudors claim the throne under Henry VII in 1485 we see Colton in the hands of three main landholders, the Gresleys being the major ones, the Bagots and St. Thomas's Priory. The village is a sizeable community with an active weekly market bringing people into the village from the surrounding area. We have no evidence that it has been particularly affected by the Black Death which decimated so many villages and even caused some to disappear totally. Colton appears to have been a thriving community.

Notes

1. SRO D603/A/ADD/173
2. SHC Vol 1 P.213-225
3. SHC Vol 1 P219
4. VCH Vol. 3
5. SHC Vol p195
6. SHC Vol3 P108 Assize Rolls
7. SHC. Vol I 213-225
8. SHC.Vol 1 p220Pipe Rolls
9. 6 Ed. I No.33 Parker.205
10. 11 Ed. I 1282 Parker p207
11. Gresley Chartulary Chattham Library Manchester
12. SRO. Close Rolls 1216-1217
13. SHC. Vol 14 P56
14. 17 Charles II Parker p153
15. Ric ii Parker p 6
16. SHC Vol 1 P156
17. SHC Vol 4 146,151
18. SHC. Vol VI(1) p243
19. Appendix Parke p83-4
20. SRO Subsidy Rolls 1327,1333 Parker 211-212.
21. 5HIII Parker
22. SHC. Vol 14 p211
23. SHC Vol 16 p272
24. 34 Ed I Parker p56
25. SHC. Vol9 p112
26. 15 Ed III Parker
27. 33 Ed III Ingestre Deeds.
28. 6 Ric.II Parker.
29. SHC. Vol I 1910

Chapter Five

Colton in the
Tudor Period

Colton in the Tudor Period

After the War of the Roses the country entered a more settled period under Henry VII. Colton in the period spanning the reign of the Tudor monarchs from the crowning of Henry VII to the death of Elizabeth I in 1603, remained mainly under the control of one family– the Gresleys. We saw in the last chapter how the Gresley family had consolidated their landholding in Colton by becoming owners of both the Church Manor and Colton Hall Manor. It is this family who would have controlled most of the affairs in the Parish of Colton.

They steadily became a relatively prominent family both in the affairs of the royal court in London for which they were duly rewarded with honours for their services and also in the Counties of Staffordshire and Derbyshire where they held their land. This steady rise in prominence appears to have been reflected in the improvements they made to their house and land in Colton.

We can only guess at what Colton Hall looked like when it was first built but we do have some clues as to what it may have been like in 1518. A Star Chamber court case[1] brought by brother and sister George and Anne Gresley against their elder brother and heir to the Gresley estates, Sir William Gresley, makes interesting reading. It recounts how brother and sister George and Anne Gresley were made executers of their mother's will. Whilst their mother Dame Anne Gresley was lying on her deathbed, Sir William helped by a number of local men and armed with bows and arrows and pikes; tried to seize her possessions! Sir William's brother and sister took him to court to retrieve them. At the end of the summary of the case is Dame Anne's will. As they did in those days, each of her possessions recorded in her will are itemised room by room. We therefore know that in 1518 Colton Hall consisted of – A 'Buttery'(room for storage of food and drink), a 'kitchen', a 'Balting House'(a place where meal was prepared to feed the animals), a 'Yelying House'(a place where the beer was brewed), a 'Day House'(probably the great hall in the centre of the house where all the business to do with the manor was conducted), the 'New Parlour'(probably part of a wing that had been built on to the central hall containing a more private room for the family), the 'New Chamber' (probably a bedroom over the New Parlour) and the 'Old Parlour'. For the early 16th Century this would have been a fairly sizeable house.

We also know that sometime in this period a 'New Park' that lay close to the house was either created or extended. Field names such as "Upper Park" and "Big Park" give us clues as to where it was. It appears to have extended down from the house towards the river. We have already recorded in a previous chapter that they owned an 'eerie' where swans were kept down on the river close to their water mill. They appear also to have engaged in falconry in the fields around there as well as stocking the park with deer etc.[2]

When the Gresleys' finally sold the manor in 1610 to a relative, Sir Walter Aston of Tixall; the house appears to have been further enlarged. Local legend talks of a huge timbered house with 83 rooms and many bedrooms.[3]

The other Manor in Colton, Little Hay Manor, still belonged to the Bagot Family. They too appeared to have built a better house sometime during this period. The pencil sketch made of this house before it was pulled down to make way for the present Little Hay Manor House; shows a Tudor timbered building. The Tudor chimneys of this house are still preserved in the garden of the present house.

MANOR HOUSE (LITTLE HAY).

The Grange in Colton owned and farmed by St. Thomas's Priory from the mid 13th Century, was to change hands in the reign of Henry VIII as a direct result of the Dissolution of the monasteries.

Roman Catholicism was the religion of England and had been adhered to in every parish of the land since before the Norman Conquest. The Pope in Rome ruled supreme and as we have already observed, the whole of Parish life revolved around the Catholic religious calendar. Churches reflected the deep devotional life in the community. One of the very few changes that had taken place by the 16th Century was that the priest in charge would now have been able to read and write Latin as well as English. In order to avoid huge numbers of unemployed clerical scroungers, the medieval church required every ordinate to have a, title, nominally a guarantee of employment and if they were non graduate priests they were conventionally given the honorific title of "Sir" as a mark of respect. A nickname sometimes used was "Sir Lacklatin" which implied they were ignorant country priests who could not read Latin.

As the 16th Century dawned the community was still charged with the costly task of maintaining all the religious trappings in the church such as candles, plate, vestments and banners. The source of revenue for these still remained the "stores" or devotional funds raised from the income generated by the church house or ale house where all village entertainment and drinking took place. There has never been any trace of where the church/ale house may have stood in Colton.

As the church in Colton is dedicated to the Virgin Mary, one of the most important stores or funds would have been for the candles for "Our Lady's" image. This fund was usually derived from the church sheep. There would have been a small flock of sheep known as the 'church flock' distributed piecemeal to individual parishioners who became responsible for the upkeep of the sheep and handing in of fleeces after shearing. One wonders if the field at the back of Colton church may once have housed this church flock. The church may have kept cattle and beehives in a similar manner.

Another fund would have been the "Young Men's Store" which would involve bachelors of communicant age, usually from 14 years old. Its main income was from the sale of ale usually called "Grooming Ales". This Store also ran "Harrow Time" for Plough Sunday when the young men went around the village residents asking for donations. If these were not forthcoming a trick or forfeit might be played upon them.

The "Maiden's Store" would involve all unmarried girls of around 12 years of age and upwards and would also have maintained the light for the Virgin Mary the money being raised at social gatherings.

All the monies from these stores would have to be accounted for at the end of each year by the church warden of the church at an annual meeting of all parishioners. The election of this post by now would have meant every head of household being expected to serve when their time came around even the widows. Refusal to serve was a serious matter and a parishioner could be prosecuted in the ecclesiastical courts for so doing. The wardens were paid 1 penny per year for their services.

In the early part of Henry VIII's reign the king and Cardinal Wolsey mobilised the theologians to preach and write against

Martin Luther who had attacked the Catholic Church. For this Pope Leo X granted Henry the title of "defender of the faith"; a title still used by the monarchy today. This allegiance to the Catholic Church in Rome was soon to be broken and England was to experience immense religious turmoil that lasted until the next century and affected everybody living in England. This period of great religious upheaval was triggered by Henry's desire to divorce Catherine of Aragon and marry Anne Boleyn. The Pope would not agree to dissolving the marriage. Urged on by Anne Boleyn, Henry nominated Cranmer as Archbishop and once in office Cranmer pronounced the King's first marriage invalid and Henry secretly married Anne. She was crowned queen in June 1533. This caused a serious rift with the Pope.

The Bishop of Lichfield, Bishop Roland Lee, is alleged to have conducted the King's marriage ceremony. He appears to have adopted a conformist attitude to what was going on and as far as we can tell there was no opposition by the church in Staffordshire to the changes that Henry now began to make. Bishop Lee was later rewarded with land when the monasteries were dissolved.

On 24th November 1534 a piece of legislation called the "Act of Supremacy" was passed. It declared that King Henry VIII and his heirs would be the only supreme head on earth of the Church of England.

Every man over the age of 14 was required to take an oath accepting the Act. Royal Commissioners all over the country were appointed to administer the oath to all adult males.

This was the moment of revolution in religious affairs in this country. The Act transferred the power of the Pope to the King of England and formally brought to an end a thousand year old allegiance to the Holy See of Rome by the English nation.

Now began a stream of measures pushed through Parliament and aimed at dismantling the Catholic Church. The clergy appear at first to put up very little resistance and one by one the demands of the Crown were accepted. Most crucially the payment of church taxes to the papacy was outlawed and received popular support.

Clergy were commanded to teach the "Act of Supremacy" to their congregations. Generally it appeared that most of the population took this in their stride. However it is thought that many of the clergy, although now having to perform Protestant practices, were secretly against this. They would have been even less likely to have liked the clerical tax of "First Fruits and Tenths" introduced in 1535 and designed to create a new royal source of revenue and taken from every beneficed cleric's income.

With Henry's rule over the English church established, the king set about the dissolution of the monasteries. His motivation for this appears to have been a desire to win political support in the country as well as to restore his financial position. The monastic lands were seized by Henry and the monasteries and priories stripped of all their possessions. Monks and nuns were made homeless. Nuns were particularly enraged by this and took to the streets proclaiming that their chief work had been to help the poor. Much of the land was given to Henry's supporters and many became wealthy.

It was at this time that the Grange Farm in Colton which had belonged to St. Thomas's Priory in Stafford was given by

Henry to Bishop Lee who in turn gave it to his nephew. In 1563 it was sold to Sampson Boughey who gave the farm the name it is still known by today. The Boughey family played a prominent part in Colton village affairs until the late 17th Century.

In 1536 Cromwell introduced the "Act of Convocation" that began to dismantle many of the practices that had been observed in the churches for centuries. Holy days were abolished with the exception of those celebrating the Virgin, the Apostles, St George, the Nativity of St. John the Baptist and All Saints' Day. He proclaimed that the profusion of Saints' days had damaged the economy because the population had not worked on Saints' days. Services could still be held on these days but work was not to be stopped. This caused widespread discontent because at a stroke Cromwell had abolished major regional festivals which were the most important social events as well as religious celebrations. They had been a source of regional pride and occasions for fairs and markets which were crucial to local communities.

These injunctions also required parents to teach their children and servants if they had any; the Lords Prayer, Creed and Ten Commandments in English rather than in Latin. More importantly it attacked the alleged superstitions surrounding the Cult of Images and pilgrimages so much part of the every day old practices throughout the kingdom. Every priest was to provide a bible in Latin and English to be placed in the church for everyone who wished to read it. Steadily the mystique surrounding the ceremonies within the church was being swept away.

In 1536 discontent with these changes caused a protest known as the "Pilgrimage of Grace" which spread through much of northern England. It was an open rebellion that came close to toppling the Tudor monarchy before it was suppressed in the spring of 1537.

The further dismantling of shrines and pilgrimage sites continued throughout 1537 and 1538. In 1538 Cromwell brought in even more strict injunctions. The clergy and parishioners were required to provide and set up the newly approved "Great Bible". Also from now on every parish priest was to keep a register of baptisms, weddings and funerals. The priest was to fill in a register every week in the presence of the church wardens. This record was to be kept in a parish chest with two locks and keys one to be held by the head church warden and one to be held by the priest.

Priests were instructed to preach a sermon at least once a quarter declaring the Gospel of Christ in which they were to tell people of charity, mercy and faith and not to subscribe any longer to or worship idolatry in any way as performed previously. This meant that the "stores" or lamp funds would steadily disappear and no new candles were to be bought except for the light before the High Cross and the Sepulchre. Money raised from the church sheep was now to be held in the accounts to be used on systematic equipping of the church in accordance with all new injunctions. The church in Colton would have had to spend 13/4d on Cramer's Great Bible, together with approximately 16d carriage from Lichfield. The string and canvas in which the book was carried would have been thriftily sold again. They were threatened with a fine of 40 shillings per month for every month they were without the Bible, a huge amount for the times. The church would also have had to pay three shillings for a book of the New Testament in English and Latin. Also 12d for a book in which to record baptisms, weddings and funerals.

There would also be the expense of buying six boards, probably old wood which had been used before, to make the church chest in which to keep the register. Nails and hinges would cost 10d, a further 12d for a villager to make the chest and 18d for two locks. Colton still has its Parish Chest.

The last years of Henry's reign seemed to be a calm after the storm of the 1530's. Colton like everywhere else would have been forced to adapt itself to the changes. The calm however was deceptive as the churches would have been almost bankrupt owing to the lack of money once freely given by villagers to their "stores" for church maintenance. Church houses did not however disappear and remained still the centre for celebrations of villagers and where the parish drank together and shared all its joys and sorrows.

The King after years of wars had caused the country to be in a state of ruination. The result was a period of heavy taxation for the people and all over England towns and villages were increasingly obliged to provide men and weapons to keep armies marching. The Parish as well as paying for the day to day running of the church also had to set aside money "in readiness for the King".

In December 1545 a Chantry Law was passed whereby monies left in trust to a chantry was confiscated. All chantry priests were pensioned off and any capital went towards Henry's War Fund.

Henry died in January 1547.

Edward VI

The new boy King Edward VI was an ardent Protestant and a further series of changes was about to be unleashed on England.

In 1547 injunctions now banned all lights or candles anywhere in the church except the two on the High Altar. Rosaries were not to be prayed upon, all processions banned, all images as well as those in stained glass windows were to be removed. Every church was to have a triple-locked chest with a hole in the top to serve as a poor man's box and the priest was to urge and encourage people on their death bed to leave money to the poor. We can see this in the Colton will of Joanne Bate of 1578. (Appendix)

In 1547, Commissioners armed with a draconian set of enquiries started to move into the regions and the process of enforcement began. When the church "stores" were closed this sudden amputation of a parish institution caused by religious reform touched not only the parish economy but a way of life which people had followed for centuries. The prohibition of ales was the closure of an important source of the social life of the village. The shared feasting linked to religious festivals was a link to village life. The contents of the church house would now have to be sold to gain any money needed by the church. However some of the church goods may have been spirited away at this time because quite a few reappeared again in the reign of Mary Tudor.

An introduction of inventories of church goods also followed. The cost to the church would probably have been 3/8d for the making of the official inventory on parchment and also having it formally agreed and sealed. We have a copy of this for Colton.

"Fyrst, one chales of silver with a patent, two vestments, two old copes. Item– Two old towlls, a cross of laten, two altar clothes, one surplus. Item– two iron kandelsticks, two bells in the stepull, a sanctus bell, and a bucket of brasse". Memorandum "Delyvered by the Rt. Honble, Walter Viscount Hereford, Lord Ferrers and of Chartley, Sir Edward Aston, Kt., and Edward Lyttleton, Esqre., Commissioners within the County of Staffordfor church goodes, to Thomas Gallande and John Wyggen churchwardens of Colton., a chalice of silver with a patent, two bells and a saunce (sanctus bell rung at mass) bell in the steeple, two linen clothes for T' holy Communion table, a surplus for the curat, savely to be kept until the King's majesties pleasure therein be further knowen: In witness whereof the aforesaid have subscribed their names". 4th May 7 Edward VI AD 1553.[4]

Before long the parishes were stripped bare of any catholic reference. Its images and ritual furnishings were gone. Its social life was suspended as the church house lay empty and every one of its parish organisations had been dissolved and the church flock sold. Taxes got worse with the introduction of a poll tax on sheep and a tax on woollen cloth which at that time was what most peoples clothes were made of unless you were very wealthy and could afford silk.

There was discontent throughout the land. A major grievance would have been the end of mass every Sunday which was much valued for healing and defence against evil spirits. The banning of baptisms on weekdays added to this resentment. This was an age when one child in ten died before they were a year old and 10% of infant mortality occurred within the baby's first week. The common belief was that delayed burial put a child's soul in danger. The Privy Council also ordered the removal of all altars and instead a table was to be set up in the chancel for communion.

All these decrees were enforced by constant visitations and inspections from the church authorities and people were too frightened to speak out against what was happening. When the final inventories of Edward's reign took place there would have been very little of value contained in the parish church. All but a single bell was allowed in churches as bells could have summoned people to rebellion. In practice this meant the removal of the clappers. However, at a later date they were allowed to buy clappers back at a price of 26/8d, causing even more financial losses to the parish. The authorities soon came to realise parishes could not survive without the sale of ales, although the church houses were by now probably sold or rented out. The sale of ales was again allowed.

In 1552 a new Book of Common Prayer was published the only legal liturgy in the Church of England and the basis for the 1662 Book of Common Prayer.

Edward VI died in 1553.

Mary Tudor

Mary was crowned in 1553. Mary was the daughter of Henry's first wife, Catherine of Aragon. Like her mother she was a devout Catholic. Upon her succession she set about dismantling the Church of England and taking the church back to Rome. With this came at least a part restoration of the Catholic faith and its rituals but by now there were many Protestants in England.

Mass was reintroduced in 1553. Many priests who had married during Edward's reign were now ejected from their livings and a large number put away their wives, did public penance, found another benefice and practiced the catholic religion again although many secretly consorted with their wives behind closed doors. It was a very confused time. Mary reintroduced the old Latin liturgy alongside the still legal Book of Common Prayer. Parishioners once more started giving money freely to the church.

Easter week of 1554 was a formal celebration of the parochial life as it was in pre Edwardian times with a spirit of devotion. A mass book was again in use and the High altars were rebuilt in churches all around the country. All the old Easter celebrations were observed, particularly the ringing for the newly dead. By 1535 the parish would have been working at full stretch to meet stringent requirements of the official Catholic restoration. Confident that the Marian restoration was here to stay they brought out any cloths and images that they had secreted away. "Stores" were reinstated to collect money for the candles and the refurbishment of the church. Craftsmen were suddenly in great demand to build new rood screens and rood lofts and to repaint all the church decorations. Also the Marian authorities now required two altars, a High Altar and one side altar designed to re-establish the cult of the saints.

Ordinary people who spoke out against the Catholic doctrines were labelled heretics and traitors and about 300 Protestants including the Archbishop of Canterbury and two other bishops were burnt at the stake. Many of the priests told their congregations that the return of Mary and the catholic faith was the advent of a good ruler. However all this was short lived as after five years the Queen was dead.

On Advent Sunday 1558 the country celebrated the accession of Queen Elizabeth I with a typical Catholic Church service. Afterwards there would have been a bonfire at the church gate with a dole of bread, cheese and beer for the poor folk of the parish. However with this Catholic ceremonial they were infact celebrating the funeral rites of Catholic England.

Elizabeth I 1558-1603.

It was vital that the new Queen signalled her religious intentions to avoid a perilous international crisis. If she retained the Catholic religion it would preserve the alliance with Catholic Spain whose help she need in continuing conflict with France and Scotland.

However Elizabeth's personal religious preference was with Protestantism. Also her best supporters were all Protestants and she could not afford to abandon them. The Marian policy had been submission to Rome and subservience to Spain but Elizabeth was her father's daughter and intent on a break with Rome. She felt that the wholesale destruction of Catholiscm would create immense problems. An example would be "Blessings" at sowing time, which might be condemned by contemporary Protestants but at the same time gave a sense of tradition to the ordinary man for whom crop failure meant something worse than hunger. Also to follow any extreme form of Protestantism would alienate Philip II of Spain and might push him into an alliance with France. Therefore all the signals she gave showed her adherence to the milder form of Protestantism.

In 1559 Parliament presented new "Bills of Supremacy and Uniformity" aimed at severing connections with Rome and endowing the monarch with the title Supreme Governor (not Head as her father had used) of the Church of England. Whilst the New Testament clearly excluded a woman from performing a spiritual ministry there was nothing to prevent her from acting as an overseer of the church. The Act also sought to repeal the Marian laws of heresy. She accepted obedience and not instruction from her bishops. To stop the Catholic Bishops and nobility opposing any bills that tampered with Catholicsm, she broke their stranglehold by reducing their numbers in the Upper House.

The new Act required the use of a Book of Common Prayer in all churches and provided a system of punishment for those who failed to use it. The Act also included the obligation to attend church on Sundays and Holy days under pain of a fine of one shilling for every absence. Parliament also transferred from the Papacy to the crown the right to claim the taxes known as "First Fruits and Tenths" from the clergy. The laity were in favour of this as they were more disposed to see the crown's income raised in this way, rather than having to contribute more themselves. Slowly the refurbishing of the churches went ahead. Communion tables were reintroduced. In 1561 a board had to be hung on a wall above the communion table with the Lord's Prayer, Creed and Commandments written on it.

In 1570 all the old ornaments had to be dismantled and sold. The remaining relic of popery would have been the chalice. The chalices had to be taken to the local Royal Commissioners and churches would be required to sell them. The price would have been in the region of 53 shillings depending on its condition.

The possessions of the church now began to look a little different. The priest would no longer have a seat to sit on whilst he preached but now had a pulpit. The books would be attached by chains and the church chest held the parish registers and records of the poor. There would be a communion table probably covered with a decent silk carpet made from a set of old High Mass vestments, surplus for the clergy and a prayer desk at the choir door. In other words the churches would have looked a lot plainer.

The parish now steadily acquired a lot more fiscal, military and administrative responsibilities. Records that had been recorded in the past by saints days now had to be recorded in secular time.

As the century came to an end it closed a period of English history marked by huge religious turmoil. Politically and economically Elizabeth marked herself out as one of the shrewdest monarchs ever to sit on the throne of England. At the time of her accession in 1558 the country was riven with deep religious divisions. At the end of the century the Church of England with its protestant practices was firmly established as the religion of the state with the monarch at its head. It would remain so through to the present day. The parishes had experienced a religious upheaval that must have had them wondering what was going to happen next. However they endured it all and ended the century with the institution of the parish holding more responsibilities to the community than ever before.

The names of the priests in Colton who oversaw this period of upheaval were 1500-1544 George Tatton. 1544-1558 John Wilson. 1558-1573 Thomas Tatton. 1573-1592 Roger Rowe. 1592- John Sanders M.A.

Notes

1. Gresley versus Gresley 1518 S.H.C. Vol 1910 S.R.O.
2. Colton and the de Wasteneys Rev. F. Parker. Private Publ. 1897 W.S.L.
3. As Above.
4. As Above.

Chapter Six

Colton in the
17th Century

Colton in the 17th Century

The 17th Century was to witness a civil war and more religious strife. Again no part of England would remain untouched by either.

At the turn of the 17th Century Elizabeth I was still on the throne although she was nearing the end of her life. Even after she had ruled for so long there were still threats to her reign, one of which in 1601 involved a Colton resident.

The second Earl of Essex had long been a favourite of Elizabeth's but in 1601 he attempted to bring about an armed rebellion against the Queen's advisors. One of his supporters was his friend Anthony Bagot who resided in Colton, at Little Hay Manor. The Essex rebellion came to nothing through lack of popular support and Essex was executed together with his stepfather for promoting it. Anthony Bagot was fortunate to escape the same fate and was pardoned in 1602. After Anthony's death his nephew went to live at Little Hay Manor. His will (see appendix on wills) was written there and gives us some clue as to what the house was like.

Colton still consisted of the two manors, Colton Hall Manor and Little Hay Manor as well as a number of large farms. The main landowners in the village remained the Bagot family at Little Hay, the Gresleys at Colton Hall and the Bougheys at Boughey Hall Farm. There was also another large house known as Wilderley on the north western edge of the parish although we know nothing of when this was built.

Life in the village would remain relatively untroubled for a number of years at the start of the century. We know something of some of the farms and their occupants from wills of the period that fortunately have survived and are held at Lichfield Record Office. The wills itemised all their possessions both outside and inside their houses. Most of the smaller farmers had a few cows and calves, a horse together with perhaps a few sheep and a couple of pigs. They would also keep hens and geese. Their farming equipment would include a plough and a cart. Inside the house all items would be listed room by room. (See appendix on wills)

The beginning of the century saw the passing of the Poor Law and Overseers were appointed in each Parish as Parish officers to make sure that money for the poor was collected from those residents who could afford to pay and then distributed to the poor of the village. The appointment was for the year and added another role to the numerous tasks the Parish officers by now were obliged by law to carry out. It is known from the Hearth Tax records of 1666 (a tax levied on households for the number of chimneys they had) that fourteen households were relieved from paying out of the sixty five assessed. It could be assumed that these fourteen were amongst those who were the poorest in the village and would benefit from poor relief.[1]

Elizabeth died in 1603. She was succeeded by James VI of Scotland who became James I of England. Thomas Gresley of Colton Hall, in his position of High Sheriff of Staffordshire and later of Derbyshire, rode to greet James on his way from Scotland to London and was duly knighted by the new king at Worksop in 1603 for his loyal service.

Religious faith was soon again to play a crucial role in events. It was still a period when freedom to practise a denomination that was not approved of by the state, was unlawful. This lack of tolerance, particularly of the Catholic faith, was to pervade the whole of this century. Those who continued to adhere to the Catholic faith were forced to carry out their religious practices in secret. There were many families in Staffordshire who remained loyal to the Catholic Church. They were ministered to by Catholic Jesuit priests who would often reside in the house of a major Catholic family in an area. These priests, trained on the continent, entered England secretly and then lived under an alias. They would not only serve their host family but also other Catholics in the vicinity, moving around constantly with the ever present danger of being caught and imprisoned or even put to death.

When James came to the throne the Catholics of England hoped that he would show some religious tolerance to them but it soon became clear that their situation was not going to change. In 1605 a number of Catholics disappointed and displeased with the attitude of the King and Parliament, sought to destroy them both. The "Gunpowder Plot", as it is known, came to nought when Guy Fawkes was discovered, along with a considerable number of barrels of gunpowder, in the cellars of the Houses of Parliament on November 5th. Those involved fled from London with the exception of Guy Fawkes who was arrested. The majority of the conspirators made their stand at Holbeach House in South West Staffordshire. All of them lost their lives, some being shot at Holbeach House whilst the rest were executed in London. This failed plot made it even more dangerous for Catholics throughout the country and created a situation of paranoid fear of Catholics that would cause some considerable difficulty not least for some Colton residents as the century unfurled.

In 1610 Walter Aston of Tixall purchased the Colton Hall Manor from his relatives Thomas and George Gresley.

Lord Aston

With this sale the Gresley family ceased their involvement with Colton after 250 years. By now Colton Hall was a substantial house. Walter Aston paid £16,000 pounds for the house and manor estate, a considerable sum for the time reflecting the size and value of the estate. Walter mixed in Royal court circles and in 1611 was created a Baronet. He served as joint Ambassador to Spain for James I between 1620 and 1625. In 1627 he was created Lord Aston of Forfar for his services to King James. Again he was in Spain between 1635 and 1638 but this time as sole ambassador and his son Herbert served with him as his secretary. We know from his letters that he was resident some times at Colton when he was at home in England. It was during this second period in Spain that he converted to Roman Catholicm and the rest of his family followed suit. There were many restrictions imposed on known Catholics and after Lord Aston's death in 1639, his widow and the family suffered many years of severe financial penalties because of their faith.

We have no evidence as to when Colton Hall was enlarged but it was probably before Walter Aston bought it and was probably one of the reasons why he purchased the estate. Oral tradition held that it was a large timber framed building reputed to have up too eighty rooms[2] and would certainly befit Walter Aston's position as an ambassador.

What is also clear from letters[3] is that his time acting for the King in Spain impoverished him greatly. At the end of his life, whilst his first son inherited Tixall and the bulk of the Colton estate, he could only afford to give his second son Herbert, who had served with him in Spain, a small estate of land in Colton. Herbert and his new wife Katherine built a house on this land that they named Bellamore (later the spelling changed). Herbert had a small secret chapel built in the house. There are no records of baptisms of children from Catholic Colton families from this period.

An artist's impression of the first Bellamore Hall

From letters written after his wife's death it would appear that Herbert and Katherine lived a happy life with their children until Katherine died in 1655.[4] Herbert and his children continued to reside at Bellamore with the exception of one daughter who went to the convent of Louvain in France where her maternal aunt was the Abbess.

Herbert's younger brother John was given property by his father at Newlands in Colton. In the 'Hearth Tax' of 1666 John was assessed as having four hearths and Herbert was assessed as having ten hearths. Richard Bagot at Little Hay had four.[5]

Sometime in the early 1650's Colton Hall burnt down reputedly because of the carelessness of a servant[6]. In 1658 the second Lord Aston sold the estate together with the water mill on the Trent to William Chetwynd of Hagley Park in Rugeley.

The other major landowners in Colton besides the Bagots and the Astons, were the Bougheys. Sampson Boughey had bought the estate in the 16th century. He was succeeded by his son George and George in turn by his son Sampson. As important members of the community both George and later his son Sampson are recorded as carrying out many duties in Colton and they also witnessed a number of wills for neighbouring farmers. The wife of the later George is recorded as being a Catholic in Catholic records but we have no idea if the whole family was.[7]

During the Civil War 1642-59, there was much activity in Staffordshire. Lichfield, Burton and Stafford were often at the forefront of the action. The Battle of Hopton Heath, north of Stafford, was fought in 1643. The victors on that occasion were the Royalists. Soon however Stafford fell, just as Lichfield already had, to the Parliamentary forces. The second Lord Aston was involved in the defence of Lichfield. As a Royalist he was imprisoned for a while in Stafford.

As to how much the Civil War affected Colton, we have no record. We do know however that the villagers had to pay money levied by Parliament on Colton and the surrounding villages to help pay for the war.[8] Often families would be split by the war. We also know that there was much troop movement by both sides all around this area and garrisons would often make camp close to villages and farms where they then demanded sustenance. Few parts of Staffordshire could have been unaffected.

Staffordshire was to feature again during the following three years with Royalist hopes to reinstate Charles (son of Charles I) as the monarch. These hopes were soon dashed in 1651 following the defeat of the future King Charles II at the Battle of Worcester. Fleeing the battle brought the future king into Staffordshire.

Having to hide in order to avoid Parliamentary soldiers who were in hot pursuit, he was concealed by a succession of Royalist Catholic supporters in various houses to the north of Wolverhampton in the area around Brewood. Thomas Whitgreave was one such Catholic and he successfully hid the future king in a priest hole at his house, Old Moseley Hall as the soldiers searched all around the immediate area. A few years later Thomas Whitgreave was to feature in events concerning Colton. Charles's final escape from the country was made possible by the help of the Lane family of Bentley Hall near Walsall. When in 1666 he became King of England at the restoration of the monarchy he rewarded all those who had aided him in his escape, including Thomas Whitgreave.

At the Restoration of the monarchy Catholics remained deprived of religious toleration. England was still very suspicious of a Catholic bid to seize the throne. This fear was once again fuelled in 1679 by claims of yet another plot to kill the king by disaffected Catholics. This plot directly implicated people in Colton. A character called Titus Oates, who somehow had the ear of various people in power at court, maintained that again there was a plot by a number of leading Catholics to dispose of the King and put a Catholic monarch in his place. Amongst those he implicated were Herbert Aston of Bellamore Hall, his nephew the third Lord Aston and their friend Lord Stafford. Titus Oates had been contacted by Stephen Dugdale who had been steward to Lord Aston but had been sacked for suspected fraud and embezzlement. Dugdale had met with a barber, John Morrall, at the White Horse in Rugeley to hatch revenge on Lord Aston. They claimed that they had overheard a plot to kill the king.

Titus Oates

Dugdale offered Morrall £50 to swear against the implicated Staffordshire men. It was claimed that these men met at Bellamore Hall, the Colton home of Herbert Aston, to discuss and agree the plot. Lord Stafford and Lord Aston were imprisoned in the Tower of London. In December 1680 Lord Stafford was beheaded for his supposed involvement but fortunately for Lord Aston the whole plot was revealed to be a hoax before he too lost his head. He was released sometime after.

This whole affair had repercussions for another family from Colton. In the late 1660's Constance Boughey one of the five daughters of Sampson Boughey and joint heiress to Boughey Hall Farm, married Whitehall Degge. Whitehall was the son of a distinguished landowner in nearby Kingston, Sir Simon

Degge. They had a daughter who died and then a son whom they named Simon after his grandfather. They appear to have lived at Boughey Hall Farm. Whitehall had been appointed to the Parish office of surveyor of the highways in 1659 for one year.[9] Constance and Whitehall bought out her other sisters' interests in Boughey Hall Farm for £750 and she became sole owner.[10] Sometime in the early 1670's Whitehall died and soon after Constance married Sir Thomas Whitgreave of old Mosley Hall, one of the rescuers of Charles II. She appears to have moved over to Old Moseley Hall taking her young son with her. We know this because in 1679,[11] the year when the paranoia about the Catholic threat to the monarchy was at its height again because of the supposed Popish Plot, her father in law Sir Simon Degge took her to court for the custody of her son. His grounds were that she was bringing him up in a Catholic household. She lost custody probably because of the climate of the times and she was forced to give her son up to be brought up by his grandfather.[12] Yet more victims of the lack of religious toleration in this period.

By her marriage to Sir Thomas Whitgreave the Boughey Hall Estate passed into the hands of the Whitgreave family. They become absentee landlords of a sizeable estate in Colton until its eventual sale in the 20th century.

In 1691 under James II, the Declaration of Indulgence allowed Catholics to hold office and to worship as they wished. Yet it would be well over another hundred years before they achieved complete emancipation.

We know of no structural changes to the church in Colton during the 17th century but it did witness the longest rectorship ever recorded for the parish. In 1651 the Rev.

Christopher Hunt died having served in Colton for fifty nine years. It was in his time that the registers began in 1647. The Rev. John Saunders followed him as Rector, his wife being a relative of his patron the second Lord Aston. He was succeeded by the Rev. John Taylor, the first of three Rectors of Colton to bear that name and all closely related. They were to serve at different times over a period of 150 years. During the Rectorship of the Rev. John Taylor, his nephew Walter Landor of Rugeley, purchased the patronage of Colton church in 1690.

As the century drew to a close more catastrophic events occurred. The great Fire of London wiped out a large part of the capital and an outbreak of plague spread throughout the country. As with the plague of the 14th century we have no evidence that the people of Colton suffered. More turmoil also soon followed over the monarchy. At Charles II death in 1689, he was succeeded by his brother James. James had embraced catholiscm well before he became King. It fairly quickly became apparent that he was trying to move the country back towards the Roman Catholic Church. By then England had been too long a Protestant country to accept this readily and in 1689 James was forced into exile. The Protestant William and Mary were invited to take the English throne.

By the close of the century England had witnessed civil war, the beheading of a monarch, more bitter religious strife, the great fire of London and a great plague. As we have noted nearly all of these events affected Colton in some way. Colton had also been the home of probably its most distinguished resident ever, Lord Walter Aston, albeit for a relatively short period of time.

Notes.

1. SHC Hearth Tax. S.R.O.

2. Colton and the de Wasteneys Rev. F. Parker Private Publ. 1879 S.R.O.

3. Letters of 1st. Lord Aston Tixall Collection of letters. W.S.L.

4. Tixall letters as above.

5. SHC Hearth Tax S.R.O.

6. Colton and the de Wasteneys Rev. F. Parker Private Publ. 1879 S.R.O.

7. Catholic church Records W.S.L.

8. Colton and the de Wasteneys Rev. F. Parker Private Publ. 1879 S.R.O.

9. Colton Church Wardens Records. S.R.O.

10. Erdswick's Staffordshire 1717 Ed. W.S.L.

11. Colton and the de Wasteneys Rev. F. Parker Publ. 1879 S.R.O.

12. Will of Simon Degge 5.6. 1727 L.R.O.

Chapter Seven

Colton in the
18th Century

Colton in the 18th Century

At the beginning of the 18th Century William III was on the throne and he had no direct heir. In order to protect the Protestant succession, upon William's death his late wife's sister Anne was by the Act of Succession in 1701 named as his successor. There was war against both France and Spain which was not peacefully settled until 1713. The following year Queen Anne died and she was succeeded by George, Elector of Hanover as George I. Within a year the son of the deposed James II, the Catholic "Old Pretender", made efforts to raise an army against the new king but to no avail. It would be another thirty years before another attempt to bring back a Catholic monarch would be made.

This century started with the Bellamour Estate still in the possession of the Aston family. John, son of Herbert Aston who had built the house, now resided there. John died in 1724 leaving no heir. The estate therefore reverted to the senior Aston line of the family living at Tixall and for the next forty years the Hall was left to tenants. There are records of two tenants for this period. The first was Thomas Bridgwood, a Roman Catholic priest who had previously served in several other Catholic homes in Staffordshire. He also used the surname Styche as an alias. The Styche family were prominent farmers in the area who farmed the Bellamour land. This would give him the necessary cover as Catholic priests were still not accepted by the state. The other known tenant at Bellamour at a later date in this period was Mrs. Elizabeth Landor, daughter of the first Rev. John Taylor who had served as Rector. She was the widow of Robert Landor of Rugeley and resided at Bellamour throughout her long widowhood.

The early years of this century also saw changes to other properties in Colton. The large farmhouse known as Wilderley was demolished. The Webb family who had occupied it and were a family associated with Colton for many generations, built a new house at Hamley possibly on the site of an older house.[1] A member of the Webb family, John Webb of Wiggington, left by his will "twenty shillings to be given to the poor every St. Thomas' Day forever charged on his house in Colton and the little croft adjoining".[2]

Another large house built in the very early years of this century was Colton House that still stands prominently in Bellamour Way today. There is a suggestion that it was possibly built on the site where the Church Manor house may have stood centuries before in the Norman period but we have no evidence to verify this. We have no record of precisely when Colton House was built and by whom but it was obviously someone of substance judging by its size and grandeur. It is known from records that Robert Hodgson, John Gomm, David Moilson and George Chambers were all owners at

Colton House.

various times in the first half of the century but nothing is known of them or if indeed any of them was the first owner.

The first records of substance for the house are from 1777 when Mr. William Pigott, "a gentleman of good family"[3] is noted as keeping harriers there. He was infact 11th in line to the crown, being related to Henry VII. He was married to Sophia, only daughter of Sir William Wolseley of nearby Wolseley Hall. She came with a fortune of £22,000, worth about £1.4 million in today's currency. Whilst he lived at the house William paid to have a long drain constructed that turned the lower end of the village and the road outside his house from being little better than the watercourse it had been for centuries into something that more resembled a road. In 1781 he insured his house against fire, covering it for a sum of £1600 and he received a firemark to confirm this insurance. It is still attached to the front of the house today.

Charles Edward Stuart, otherwise known as "Bonnie Prince Charlie", landed in Scotland in 1745 and established an army. He planned to march to London to reclaim the throne for the Catholic Stuarts. As they marched southwards they passed through the north of Staffordshire and moved as far as Derby before they realised that the army of George II was approaching northwards. Both the Scots and the would-be-king retreated to Scotland followed by the King's army. This army passed through Rugeley and plundered Hagley Hall before continuing their pursuit. There were many English people who supported the Jacobite cause (the claim of Charles Stuart to the throne). One of these was the then Rector of Colton the Rev. John Taylor who found himself in Stafford Goal in 1751 for declaring his support for Charles

Stuart. By that time the English army had severely and cruelly defeated the Scots, their leader had fled to the continent never again to set foot in the land of his ancestors.

We know of major changes that were made to the church building during this Century. Two of the present bells were hung in the bell chamber in 1704 and in 1791. Right at the end of this century the original north aisle was taken down because of its ruinous state and a new brick north wall was constructed. It is possible that the roof was also renewed at this time because there is evidence from the churchwardens accounts that a substantial amount of oak timbering was purchased for the church at for those days the considerable cost of £117.19.6d[4] The windows within the new brick wall were round headed in the fashion of the day and were therefore significantly different from the early English style of the remaining windows.[5]

Colton St. Mary's. A sketch showing what the church looked like in the 18th. Century.
Sketch in F. Parker. Colton and the de Wasteneys

Another charity is also established in this period. – The "Good Friday Dole". Mrs. Mary Taylor, daughter, sister and Aunt of three successive Rectors of Colton ("Mrs." was a courtesy title) left by her will dated the 2nd April 1755 the sum of £25, to purchase land. Part of the rent, £1, was to be distributed to those who attended both morning and evening services on Good Friday. Rent from this land also partially paid the salary of the head teacher at the new Free School that was established in the village in 1764 (See chapter on education in Colton.)

Colton Charity Board in Colton Church.

Also in the second half of this century two changes occurred that were to dramatically affect the landscape around Colton. The first was due to the steady industrialisation of England. Natural resources in the Midlands area were now being exploited by the rapidly developing iron, coal and pottery industries. As demand intensified, improvements in the means by which materials could be transported cheaply and safely around the country became paramount. Horses and carts could not cope on the appalling roads of England. This resulted in rich landowners and a new class of factory owners like Josiah Wedgwood at Stoke on Trent and the brewers at Burton on Trent, forming companies to build, run and profit from a new form of canal transportation. There was a meeting held at Wolseley Bridge in December of 1765 to discuss the building of a canal. James Brindley was commissioned to create the waterway running from Preston Brook (Runcorn near Liverpool) to Shardlow near Derby, thus linking the River Mersey and the River Trent. This made it possible for boats to travel from Liverpool in the west to Hull in the east. The 93 mile long Trent and Mersey Canal was constructed between 1766 and 1777 and came through Colton.

This canal passes through the western edge of the Parish and includes a Brindley designed bridge and a winding hole (for the turning of boats) and also a private wharf, possibly for the Bellamour Estate. As the canal leaves the parish boundary it is carried over the River Trent by a Brindley designed aqueduct.

The second great change to affect the landscape in the second half of this century was the enclosure of fields brought about by the Enclosure Acts of Parliament. Land had been enclosed (a land owner bringing his pieces of land together in a block rather than having them scattered around the village) in previous centuries and usually by agreement amongst local landowners. Despite these earlier enclosures as much as half the existing arable land still lay in open fields. The Enclosure Acts that began in the latter half of the 18th century allowed the larger landowners within a village to legally enforce enclosures on those open fields that remained. They were prompted by many innovations within farming with new crops such as turnips being grown, new machinery for sowing and threshing being introduced and new breeds of cattle, sheep and pigs being developed by animal experimentation. Landowners quickly realised that the productivity of an enclosed farm could be significantly greater than the open field system of strips that had existed for centuries. An enclosed farm was easier to work and rotation on a larger scale increased the yield on the land. Former common or waste land which had been used by all the community was now being brought into use as part of the larger farm unit. Large scale farms became highly profitable. Landlords also often used enclosure as an opportunity to raise rents and average rents almost doubled in this period. Those who suffered most were the small farmers, squatters and farm labourers who had historically relied heavily on low rents and communal grazing land.

Although oxen were still used to haul the ploughs, the use of the heavy horse became more prevalent. The Shire horse was the main breed in this locality for this task. It is known that the Styche family, mentioned earlier as farming the Bellamour estate lands, were nationally renowned for their contribution to the improvement of the Shire horse breed.

In the last decade of the century by private Act of Parliament the wastes, heaths and commons were enclosed in Colton by Lady Mary Blount who now owned the Bellamour Estate and resided there. She did this along with 18 other landowners who held land in Colton. However they were philanthropic.

*A building from this period in Colton, a threshing barn,
is still preserved today. It was rescued in a state of dilapidation
from a farm in Colton a few years ago and was completely
rebuilt and restored and now stands at Wolseley Bridge.*

Following the Act a charity known as the "Colton Parish Lands
Trust" was formed. This Charity still functions today for the
benefit of the people of Colton. Some of the common land
was sold to provide funds to create hedges and fences and
also to build six almshouses at Stockwell Heath that became
known as "The Barracks"

Those who had built houses in the past on the common lands
at Stockwell Heath and in Hollow Lane were able to remain
living in them but had to now pay rent. The enclosed land
now divided into fields was rented out. The money raised was
to be used first to defray costs and then afterwards the profits
were for "the relief and maintenance of the poor of Colton
Parish and in aid and ease of the Poor's Rate". Two marl pits

were to remain for use by the parishioners to extract marl to spread on their fields. This 1792 Act of Parliament also set up a Board of Trustees to oversee the working of the Charity.

Alms houses affectionately known as The Barracks at Stockwell Heath built to house the poor of the parish.

The Blount family had come into possession of the Bellamour Estate in 1766. In 1751 the fifth Lord Aston had died leaving two young heiresses and his estates were divided between them. Barbara, the younger daughter received the Tixall Estate and Mary, the elder, inherited the Bellamour Estate. In 1766 Mary married Sir Walter Blount at the home of their relative, the Duchess of Norfolk, at Worksop in Nottinghamshire. Mary's husband died in 1785 and following this she spent much of her time at Bellamour.

Around 1796 she had a second much larger house built next to the first for her second son Edward Blount. At the same time a new road was created to give more privacy to the house and to enlarge the parkland.

A picture of Mary Blount extracted from a painting exhibited at Burton Constable Hall.

The two houses at Bellamour from an illustration in "Colton and the de Wasteneys" by Rev. F. Parker.

Until then the road from Rugeley turned across the present parkland skirting around the old hall to emerge at the area known today as Bellamour End.

Lady Blount was to suffer vandalism in her new park. Trees were uprooted and anti-Catholic slogans were erected. (The family had remained Catholic). However she did not take any action and those who had endeavoured to persecute her soon gave up. A chapel was included in the new hall like its predecessor in the old hall. Like its predecessor the new hall became a centre for local catholic families and many Roman Catholic baptisms are recorded in the register. The Bellamour baptism register dates from 1792 and is kept amongst the Catholic church records at St. Chad's Roman Catholic Cathedral in Birmingham.

Another new road was created at this time through the Bellamour Estate lands at the Newlands. Historically the roadway had continued along what was known as 'Bowling Alley Lane' and 'Mere Lane' to the hamlet of Newlands. A new section of 'Newlands Lane' was cut across the fields to make the journey more direct.

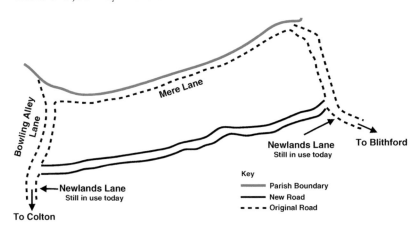

In 1792 John Heylinger Burt purchased Colton House. He was one of the landowners and trustees involved in the Act of Parliament to enclose the waste and common land around Colton so that it could then be sold or rented out to raise money for the relief of the poor of Colton. John married Judith the daughter of the Rector of nearby Maveysn Ridware. She had been married before to one of the Okeover family of Osmaston in Derbyshire. Judith's great grand- daughter was a maid of honour at Queen Victoria's wedding. John's father's family were very rich and had great influence in many of the Caribbean islands, where the family had held many influential posts. The family were connected on his mother's side, the Heylinger family, to two USA presidential families, the Adam's and the Roosevelt's.

John had inherited sugar plantations on Saint Croix and the family had strong connections with the slave trade. At the end of the 18th Century they were living in Colton house where they raised four children.

At the end of the century England was poised to enter the most prosperous and influential period in its history. There is every indication that Colton was participating in the many changes that were taking place and that it was far from being in a backwater. The landscape in Colton had been altered by the enclosures, large residences had been erected and roadways moved. Colton was positioned on one of the national networks of communication and narrow boats hauled by horses making their way along the Trent and Mersey canal would be a very common feature. Its landowners were progressive and the village occupants were about to take advantage of the many opportunities that were going to arise from the new industries that would flourish in the surrounding area in the next century.

Notes.

1. Colton and the de Wasteneys by Rev. Parker. Private Publ. 1897 S.R.O

2. Webb Trust Papers. Colton School Trust.

3. Colton and the de Wasteneys as above

4. Churchwardens' Accounts D 570/a/173 S.R.O.

5. Colton and the de Wasteneys as above.

Chapter Eight

Colton in the
19th Century

Colton in the 19th Century

As the new century dawned England was once more at war with France. Victory at sea came in 1805 at the great Battle of Trafalgar but it would be another ten years before the final battle at Waterloo in June 1815 which brought an end to the war. George III was on the throne until 1820 albeit that his son, the future George IV acted as regent for many years because of his father's periods of madness.

The people of Colton would probably have been little affected by these national events and certainly for the first half of the century little would change in the village. It was in the long reign of Queen Victoria that began with her coronation in 1837 that the industrialisation of Britain took place, bringing with it many changes that would affect all communities in one way or another.

It was a tragic local event that probably mattered more to the villagers at the beginning of the century. In 1805 the people of Colton heard of the death of the lady of Bellamour Manor, Lady Mary Blount, in a horrific accident. Although she lived at Colton she was staying at her youngest son's home at Basford in Staffordshire when a spark from the fire alighted on her dress. Lady Mary died from burns on 30th January 1805.[1] The Bellamour estate then came into the ownership of her second son Edward who came with his family to reside in the new Bellamour Hall until 1824. His sons received their early education at Rugeley Grammar school. They rode to school on donkeys accompanied by a servant.[2]

Little Hay was still in the ownership of the Bagot family and remained so throughout the century. Boughey Hall Farm did not change ownership and remained in the hands of the

Whitgreave family throughout this century. Both of these large farms were still tenanted. In 1828 the Colton Hall Estate was sold, having been held for two hundred years by the Chetwynd family of Rugeley. Lord Anson of Shugborough was the purchaser of Colton Hall and he installed tenants on the estate. Three years earlier in 1825 fourteen small lots around the village were sold at auction including a beer house, the Dun Cow and a small farm in the centre of the village known as the Malthouse. The purchaser of the Malthouse was another absentee landlord, Admiral Tatham (1846 tithe Award). This meant that of the larger properties in the village only the Bellamour Estate was occupied by its owners. The villagers still looked to this family residing here as being the 'lords of the manor of Colton' and they remained the most important family in the village both in terms of influence and employment.

The Church continued to be the hub of village life and its upkeep remained an important issue. The major repair works on the church mentioned in the last chapter were completed with the installation of a gallery for the singers to occupy at about 1812. Before this time the Rector, the Rev. John Landor was rebuked by the church wardens for using the belfry as a pigeon loft and his nephew and successor the Rev. Charles Savage Landor, not surprisingly, was not allowed to continue the practice when he became rector![3]

John Landor, on becoming Rector of Colton, had taken up residency in the Rectory. The Rectory at this time was sited where the new Rectory stands today at the side of the Moreton Brook with the old tithe barn standing in front of it. He regarded the proximity of the house to the brook as responsible for the deaths of seven of his children and because of this he had spent many of the later years of his life residing in the family home in Rugeley. On a site to the east of the church and a sufficient distance from the brook, he had a new Rectory built in 1806 but never lived there (the present day "Old Rectory"). His successor the Rev. Charles Savage Landor became Rector of Colton in 1806 on the death of John Landor and took up residency in the new house. Some seventy years later the Rectory was enlarged. The house you see today is somewhat smaller because the servants' quarters were demolished in 1956.

The Rectory built in 1806

The tithe barn situated close by the entrance to the church drive was still used to hold the Rectors' tithes of $\frac{1}{10}$ of all crops grown on the tithable parts of the parish. Rev. John Landor was very diligent in collecting all of the tithes that were due to him and took a dim view of anyone who tried to avoid them.

He took his neighbour William Spencer of Boughey Hall Farm to the High Court in London in a dispute over the tithes from the farm. William Spencer had not been paying them and the Rev. Landor won his case.[4] The tithe records for Colton for this period still exist.[5]

Colton Tithe Barn.

His successor Rev. Charles Landor must also have been a man of strong principles because he also took court proceedings against his parishioners in 1815 over a footpath. It was a custom of the people walking to church from the village to make their way behind Colton House and then to pass across the north side of the newly built rectory. He strongly objected to this. He too won his case. Charles Landor died in 1849 and was succeeded by the Rev. Abdiel Seaton.

Abdiel Seaton decided that the church was in need of major repairs despite the work that had been carried out fifty years previously. A complete restoration of the building was put into the hands of George Edmund Street who was one of the most eminent church architects of this period. Street was a proponent of the Gothic Revivalist movement that flourished in this century and so his designs for the restoration of Colton Church reflected this style. For a short period William Morris, who became prominent in the Arts and Crafts movement of the latter half of the century, was one of his apprentices.

Colton church after the restoration
and as it appears today.

The nave, which included a new north aisle to replace the brick one, was rebuilt in stone using the Early English style of architecture. A new chancel and sanctuary were built and the old chapel became the modern day vestry. He preserved the original piscina and sedilia within the vestry. It was whilst they were undertaking this restoration that the 14th Century wall paintings were found under the whitewash in this part of the church. (See Chapter 4) At the time it was considered impossible to preserve them but drawings were made of what could be seen of them before they were destroyed.[6]

New furniture in wood and stone including an organ were incorporated into the building. The brick floor of the church was replaced by earthenware tiles popular in the period and the chancel and the sanctuary were tiled with products from the by now famous Herbert Minton factory in Stoke-on-Trent. Herbert Minton donated the tiles for 'the altar place' and the others were purchased.

Other gifts were given to the church over the next few years. Abdiel Seaton purchased three medieval misericords (priest's seats) that had been found in a summer house in a garden in Tenby and these were installed in the sanctuary. An extra bell was donated by Miss Ellen Oldham of Bellamour Lodge in 1852. Several stained glass memorial windows were given. In the later years of the century other memorial gifts were made. These included a larger organ installed in 1879 which incorporated the 1851 organ. A new corona was installed in the chancel in 1892 and this now hangs at the west end of the nave. The corona of 1851 can now be found in the vestry (the original chapel). Central heating piped from an external boiler house was installed at the end of the century. How welcome that must have been to those who worshipped there! This Street restoration is the church you see today in Colton.

As we have already noted Edward Blount succeeded his mother in the ownership of the Bellamour Estate and the Manor of Colton upon her death in 1805. In 1824 he sold the

May Day celebrations outside Bellamour Hall.

Bellamour estate and with this sale came to an end a lineage that had commenced with the de Wasteneys some 700 years before. The estate was purchased by James Oldham Oldham, a retired judge who had previously practised in India. His wife and daughters came to live in Colton. Ellen, one of his daughters who remained unmarried, held a school for girls in the old Bellamour Hall for some years where she taught them to read and to sew. In 1851 James Oldham Oldham built the substantial, elegant Bellamour Lodge at the entrance to Colton for Ellen. About 25 years later she enlarged her home on the eastern side and erected a veranda on the south side.

Bellamour Lodge.

In 1857 James Oldham died and the estate, minus Bellamour Lodge and a few fields surrounding this house, was sold. The purchaser was Thomas Berry Horsfall, Member of Parliament for Liverpool. He enlarged the estate considerably.

Thomas Berry Horsfall thoroughly involved himself in the affairs of Colton and was a generous benefactor to the Parish. He gave a portion of his land to create a cemetery and also gave land for the building of a new school and school master's house in 1862. He also donated money to finance the project (see chapter 9 on schools).

He also gave land and money so that a village meeting room known as "The Reading Room" could be built. The present day "Reading Room Drive", the access to the present village hall, was the site of this "Reading Room".

After he died his widow had a life interest in the Bellamour Estate albeit that the ownership was held by her stepson, Henry Leeke Horsfall.

Other new buildings appeared in Colton in this century. In 1846 the former Little Hay Manor House that had been there since Elizabethan days was demolished, leaving only the Tudor chimneys. They were left standing on the recommendation of Henry Walter Holland, the tenant at that time.[7] The new house and farm buildings surrounding the farmyard on three sides were built to a farmyard plan that became popular in the mid 19th century reflecting the advances in farming practice. Close by Shugborough Hall farm had been one of the first in the country to adopt this plan.

When Thomas Berry Horsfall purchased the Bellamour Estate he rebuilt the entrance lodges. The lodge on the road to Bishton was re-sited further along the road and a new entrance drive was created.

There were also a number of cottages built in this century. Some of them bear the dates either in the form of a plaque such as that on Williscroft Place or are built into the brickwork as can be seen on the side of the Clerk's House in Bellamour Way. When Ellen Oldham died in 1883, her sister Mrs. Elizabeth Harland decided to build a terrace of almshouses in her memory to house the old people of Colton. The building demolished to make way for these almshouses had been an inn known as the "Three Wheels" and later "The Bell". It had also been the site of the village stocks.

The Almshouses

The licence for the inn was transferred to a cottage opposite in Williscroft Place and this became known as "The Greyhound" and retains that name today.

A new road was also built. In the years between 1828 and 1845 a road linking the Trent Valley area of the Parish and the eastern end of Hollow Lane was constructed. It is now known as the Blithbury Road but was originally called "The New Road" (Tithe map 1845) and was referred to by this name as late as 1906. It gave access to Colton Hall and Old Wood Farm so that the cartways that had gone across to these two properties from Hollow Lane that had been used for centuries now fell out of use on a regular basis. Other footpaths were still used however to serve those walking from Rugeley towards Blithbury and Abbots Bromley.

Colton House acquired an illustrious tenant during the 1880's and someone who was to leave a photographic legacy to the village of immense value. We know little of who lived in the house in the period after the Heylinger Burt's had owned it other than in the 1841 and 1851 Census returns where it is recorded as "Colton House Academy Boarding and Day School". It was run by a Mr. Mills and there were 11 boys as boarders. The Horsfall's acquired the property and sometime in the late 1880's Frederic Bonney took up residence as their tenant. His mother, Eliza Ellen Smith, was descended from an old yeoman family named Pegg who had lived in the village since the 1500's. She had inherited a considerable amount of land in the north and north eastern part of the parish and this is possibly why he came to live here.

Frederic had followed in the footsteps of his uncle when in 1865 he left the family home in Rugeley and travelled to Australia. His Uncle Charles had been one of the early pioneer explorers in Australia opening up routes for cattle across the continent. Frederic and his brother Edward ran sheep stations north of Adelaide. He was a keen photographer in a time when photography was in its infancy and during his stay in Australia he took many pictures.

He took pictures of the new settlements, the settlers and their working activities. He also took pictures of the indigenous Aborigines making copious notes of their language and customs. He is recognised in Australia today as one of the first people to make such extensive records and his photographs and notes are now held in the Henry Mitchell Museum of

New South Wales in Sydney and in the Library in Canberra. When he came back to live in England he wrote and then read a paper on his findings about the Aborigines to an eminent audience in London and for this research he was elected a Fellow of the Royal Geographical Society.

When he moved into Colton House he became very involved in the life of the village. He became the first chairman of the newly formed Colton Parish Council and a trustee of the new village school. He also continued his photography and took many pictures of life and activities around the village. Fortunately many of these photographs survive and provide a tremendous insight into life in Colton in the latter part of the 19th Century. He moved away from Colton and back to Rugeley in 1902.

Frederic Bonney pictured with his aboriginal workers on his sheep station in Australia around the 1870's. (Collection in Mitchell Library Sydney.)

*Inside Colton House when Bonney lived there
showing his Australian memorabilia.*

Children skating on the Plantation Pool - Bonney Photo.

The 19th Century saw the development of Britain's railway system. In 1845 the "Trent Valley Railway Act" was passed by Parliament. This railway running from Stafford to Rugby would pass through the southernmost part of the Parish of Colton close to the canal. "In the spring of 1846 the landscape

The railway station at Colton.

of the Trent Valley was changing. For centuries the main activity of the valley had been agriculture but now the railway to London was under construction. Hundreds of labourers using picks and shovels were at work building a low embankment across the western edge of Bellamour Park and onwards towards the site of a new railway station. The hillside close by Colton Mill Farm would reverberate from explosions of black powder as the sandstone was blasted away. This stone would be fashioned by masons to face the locally made bricks used in building the stations and bridges".[8] On 26th June 1847 the line was officially opened and became known as the "Premier line". We can perhaps assume that James Oldham Oldham, whose land the railway passed through, was at that ceremony! Thirteen years later another line opened from the station in Colton to Cannock. It was to be another ten years before there was to be a station in Rugeley, known as Rugeley Town and the Colton station became Rugeley Trent Valley.

A station master's house and a row of houses for some of the railway workers were built close to the line. They became known as "The Fog Cottages" (1891Census). "They got their nickname from the bells being installed to call out to the men to place detonators on the line in foggy conditions to help the train drivers".[9]

The main line traffic continued to increase and the goods yard next to the station became a very busy place. The railway bought a new form of employment for people in Colton and the census records of this period show a number of residents finding employment on or around the railway system.

Industrialization was affecting many traditional trades and practices. Even Colton Mill on the river Trent that for centuries had ground corn, in 1870 was described in "the Trades Directory" for Staffordshire as now manufacturing cement and plaster of Paris, presumably for the local pottery industry. There were also brick kilns on the site providing bricks for the expanding housing market as more people moved to the towns. In 1895 the mill became the property of the Derby Oxide and Colour company Ltd. A far cry from corn!

Census records had begun at the start of the century and it is from these that we can discern the types of employment people were engaged in and who lived in Colton. As already mentioned, some gained employment on the new railways but most people were still tied to the land. There were more than a dozen large farms and several smaller ones in the parish and many residents worked in some capacity on them. Agricultural workers were by far the greatest proportion but these farms and houses also provided other forms of employment such as gardener, coachman, housemaids, cooks and others. Some gained employment in the tannery in Rugeley and later in the century the mines on Cannock Chase. The first part of the working day for people from Colton still had to be a journey by foot and the many bridleways and paths were all in constant use.

Some Colton men and their families
who worked on the railway.

Notes

1. Colton and the de Wasteneys by Rev. Parker. Private Publ. 1897 S.R.O.

2. Memories of Sir Edward Blount K.C.B. Publ. 1902

3. Colton and the de Wasteneys

4. D(W)1808/2/8 S.R.O.

5. D4813/2/80 S.R.O.

6. Colton and The de Wasteneys

7. 1891 Census Record

8. Pamphlet on Railways by David Bradbury Publ. Colton History society. 2006

9. As above

    A History of Rugeley by W. N. Landor

    A Report of the Industrial Complex known as Trent Valley Works formerly Colton mill by Tony Parkes

    Railways of the West Midlands, a chronology 1808 -1954 by Stephenson Locomotive Society.

    Records of the Herbert Minton Factory.

Chapter Nine

The History
of Education
in Colton

The History of Education in Colton

This chapter was taken from the information collected for and displayed at the 2006 Colton History Society Exhibition when the History Society featured the school as one of its main themes. Included in the exhibition was a recreation of what we think a schoolroom looked like in Colton school in the late 1890's. We were inspired by the photograph we found of Miss Mansell and her class as photographed by Frederic Bonney and referred to later in this chapter.

Amongst all the dramatic changes brought about in the 19th century, the provision of education was perhaps the most significant, and it paved the way for many of the important social, economic and demographic changes of the 20th century.

Until the great Education Act of 1870 the State did not provide education.

For centuries if parents could afford to educate their children they had to pay for it privately. The majority of the population could not afford it and received no formal education at all.

However with the coming of the Industrial Revolution in the late 18th century, the demand for a workforce who could at least read and write, began to arise. Factory owners needed their workforce to have some education in order to understand how to work the machinery. The first organisations to provide a basic education for the working classes were the Church of England and the Free Church movement. They began to run Sunday schools.

However Charities and benefactors also saw the benefit of providing education to the masses as well and it was a small group of such forward-thinking wealthier residents of Colton who decided to do something about educating the poor children of the village and surprisingly early on. The first school in Colton village opened its doors in 1765.

The First School.
"The Free School" founded 1765

This was formally established On 11th Feb 1765 when "Sir William Wagstaff Bagot of Blithfield, Robert Landor of Rugeley Esq. and John Pegg, Gent of Colton" sold to Lord Bagot (son of William Wagstaff Bagot), John Sneyd of Bishton, Walter Landor, (son of Robert Landor), the Rev Walter Bagot Rector of Blithfield, John Taylor Rector of Colton, John Pegg Junior, of Colton, John Smith of Longdon, William Emery of Colton, William Spencer of Colton, for the sum of 10/- a "newly erected dwelling and schoolhouse with garden and outbuildings".[1]

The money also purchased a close of land in Colton and several closes of land in Uttoxeter. This land was let out and the income raised, paid for - the head teacher's salary of £10 per annum. It also provided, "quills, ink and books" for the children whose parents could not afford them, fuel to heat the school and any repairs needed to the schoolhouse.[2]

It was stipulated that the head was to teach 20 children from the village. He could however take up to 20 more children to increase his income as long as it did not interfere with the 20 who were being paid for by the charity.

He was to teach "reading, writing, arithmetic and the Church of England catechism".[3] He also had to accompany the

141

children to church on Sunday and make sure that they behaved.

In 1821 John Spencer on behalf of his brother Francis Spencer who had farmed at Boughey Hall in Colton; left a Charity in the sum of £500 to be invested in order to provide more income for the running of the school. This became known as the Spencer Charity.

This first school was based in School Cottages, Bellamour Way. The building still stands today although altered somewhat.

If you look carefully at the building you can still see where the two doorways to the school were. Over the doorways was written:

"This house was converted into a school by generous contributions of the neighbours 1765"

"Train up a child in the way it should"[4]

We do not know who the first head was but we do know that an advert was placed in the Staffordshire Advertiser of 1804 for a new head. The advert read–

"A master is wanted for the Charity school at Colton to instruct 20 poor children in the English language, writing and accounts. Salary £10 per year, with a house and garden rent free, under certain restrictions as to his conduct. He will also be permitted to take any other number of children not exceeding 20 on his own account. Application to be made to the Rev. John Landor or to Messrs. Hicken & Landor, solicitors in Rugeley".

Although education at this date had not been formalised there was a voluntary inspection system on behalf of the church. In 1830 the school received this report from inspectors on behalf of the church:

"The boys and girls are taught in one room, boys at the bottom and girls at the top. The master and his son teach the boys, his wife and daughter teach the girls. They are all instructed in reading, writing, arithmetic and the church catechism. The girls are also taught to sew and knit".[5] The school was obviously run as a family affair!

The Head at this time appears to have been William Simpson who is recorded in Whites Directory of 1834 as being the head teacher on a salary of £50.00 per annum and he also acted as Parish Clerk.

Miss Elizabeth Williscroft, schoolmistress, is named on the 1841 Census as living at the schoolhouse. We have no idea if she was running the school on her own. If William Simpson was still head, which is most likely, he may have been living at the Parish Clerk's House next door.

In the 1851 census Thomas Lenton is now the head teacher helped by Thomas Gardner a schoolteacher. Mr. Lenton remained the head until 1862. This is all we know of this first school.

The Second School.
"The Webb Trust School" 1811

In 1762 Thomas Webb of Egginton, had left property in trust in Colton to provide income to educate "20 poor girls of the parish" They were to be "instructed in reading, writing and sewing".[6] In 1811 Thomas's heir John Webb, gave in his will, these properties and some additional properties and parcels of land to create a Trust. The Trust became the owners and the income derived from the properties and land ran a school that became known as The Webb School.

The property was "Three cottages known as Webb's Cottages".[7] They survived until the early 1960's. Also "The Three Wheels Pub" later became known as "The Bell" and was on the site of the present day Oldham's Cottages.

Also parcels of land in Colton including that known as "Vincent's Hollowdale".

The "Webb School" for "20 poor girls of the Parish" appears to have been held at first in one of the Webb's Cottages. This has been passed down by word of mouth i.e. local residents always called it the Webb schoolroom long after it had ceased to be used as such.

We think the school then moved into a small building which formed part of the outhouses of the rectory that used to be on the site of the present day new rectory. Again oral tradition called this "the old schoolroom".

The Webb Cottages, to the south east of the High Street,
where it is thought the school was first held.
They were demolished in the early 1960's.

The Third School. A Private "Academy" at Colton House

The only information we have on this school is from the Census records of 1851.

It appears to have been run by a Mr. Richard Mills and there are 18 Boarders recorded as living there. It cannot have lasted for long because it is not recorded on the 1861 census.

There were many private schools around the country of this type in the Victorian era. They were usually small and were used by families who had a little money to fund an education for their children.

Many of them were well run but some were not. Often unscrupulous owners would hoodwink parents into thinking that their children were getting a good education and were being well cared for. Some parents would use them as a "dumping ground" for their children, not really caring whether they were being properly cared for and educated. Charles Dickens became aware of this and focused attention on the plight of the children in such schools in his book Nicholas Nickleby. Many of the schools were subsequently closed down.

Colton House where a school was held in the 1850's

A Dickensian School Room.
We have no idea how well the one at Colton was run.

The Fourth School

A school for girls at the old Bellamour Hall run by Miss Ellen Oldham.

The Old Bellamour Hall.

We know of this school because it is mentioned by the Rev. Parker in his book about Colton and also Dorothy Bradbury, a colton resident, once was shown a "sampler" that had been done around 1835 by a girl who had attended the school. It was probably run on the lines of a "Dame School" of which there were thousands around the country in the late 19th Century before education was provided by the state and became compulsory.

Dame Schools

These were small schools often run by one female, usually untrained, who for a very small fee would offer some education. It would be reading, writing and arithmetic and possibly sewing for the girls as well. Many of Dame schools were held in the rooms of cottages and provided a meagre living for the person who ran them.

Ellen Oldham however was the daughter of the owner of Bellamour Hall, James Oldham Oldham and the Lord of the Manor of Colton. She was probably therefore doing this as an act of charity for some of the girls of Colton who were not receiving an education in either of the other two schools. She certainly did not need the money!

We do not know how long this school existed for but it is more than likely that it closed down well before the new school for all the village children was built and opened in 1862.

Free School and Webb School begin to work more closely together.

As time went on the Free School and the Webb Charity School began to work more closely together.

In 1861 the Charity Commission was asked by the then Rector of Colton Abdail Seaton and Thomas Berry Horsfall M.P. the owner of Bellamour Hall, if they would give permission for the Free School and the Webb School to be amalgamated in order to provide education for all the boys and girls of the village. This permission was given in 1862.

Thomas Berry Horsfall then provided the land and the money to build a new school and a house for the headmaster. The combined assets and income of the Webb Charity, The Free school Trust and the Spencer Charity, were to pay for the running and maintenance of the school. The school and headmaster's house, Elm Cottage, were built.

The school became known as the:- Colton United Schools.

This new school was the building you see today but it was not as big. It opened its doors officially on 19th December 1862 when "We marched from the old school and opened the new

148

The New School, photo by Frederic Bonney

school. A prayer was said By Reverend Seaton. We then broke up for Christmas".[8]

The school was to be for all the children of Colton of both sexes between the ages of 2 and 14. There was no law at this time to require the children of the village to attend but pressure will probably have been put on the parents by the Rector, Mr. Horsfall and other trustees to try and ensure that they did attend. The parents who could afford it, had to pay for their children to attend. For the few that could not pay, a village benefactor such as Miss Oldham, Mr. Horsfall or Mr Harland would pay for them.[9]

Scales of Pay for Pupils

A scale of payment was set by the Trustees on 6th June 1863.

Parents were to pay 2d for the first child 1d for each additional child.

It was revised in October 1874 to: 3d for the first child, 2d for the second, 1d for any other children.

Payment had to be made at the beginning of each week.

The first Curriculum of the New School

The Head was required to teach "Reading, writing, spelling, English Grammar, arithmetic, general history, geography and any such subjects as useful or industrial knowledge including needlework and knitting to be taught to the girls, religious knowledge comprising the bible and bible history and must be consonant with the principles and doctrines of the Church of England".[10]

Although the school was not run by the Church of England, it held to all its principles and was inspected by them. In 1866 an inspection of the school by the Diocese inspector said:

"The children are in good order. The three lowest standards have passed well in the secular subjects. The three highest standards have failed in arithmetic. The spelling too of the fifth standard needs attention. Religious knowledge is fairly good. Girls needlework improved. The registers should be marked more regularly".[11]

The Headmaster's House

The Head teacher was required to live in the village and he resided at the house built for the purpose by Mr. Horsfall, known as Elm Cottage.

The Early Head teachers

Mr. Lenton who had been the head of the free school, retired on a pension paid for from the school charities (a very good one for the time!). He was also allowed to continue to live in School Cottages.

Miss Garner, who had run the Webb School, now ran the Webb School as the infant department of the new school. She remained at the school until her retirement some years later also on a pension.

The Headmasters House, Elm Cottage in the 1930's

Mr. Dodge, was appointed and one of the requirements of his appointment was that he lived in the Headmaster's house provided. He left in 1869.

Mr. Sutton, who had taught as an assistant teacher at the school, was appointed as the head.

Assistant teachers were in effect adult trainee teachers, training on the job. They had to work for qualifications and many of the men went on to be head teachers. They were paid a lot less than the head but they were paid a reasonable salary. They were older and a lot better qualified than the pupil teachers or monitors that were in use in many Church of England schools. This system was where an older pupil was picked out to watch over and monitor what younger pupils were doing. Monitors had to be 12 years old but were often barely more literate than the pupils they were in charge of. Pupil teachers had to be 14 and had to have passed the 6th Standard.

Over the years there were assistant teachers and pupil teachers at Colton.

Mr. Sutton appears to have struggled with the headship of the school. During his time as head he has lots of problems with children not attending. He also had trouble with maintaining the standard of learning in the school. Inspection after inspection records that the standards are slipping.

1875 "The school is in a less efficient state than it was a year ago… My Lords have ordered the grant be reduced for the mixed school by one tenth for defective instruction."[12]

Grants were brought in following the 1870 Education Act when Educational provision became the responsibility of the State. A grant given to the school depended on maintaining and improving standards – a system which became known as "Payment by Results". Colton for a number of years had its grant reduced.

1890 "The results are so poor the trustees must consider a formal warning next year if the results do not improve".[13]

In fairness to Mr. Sutton the pressure upon him to come up with improving standards when a lot of the time the children were not attending because it was not compulsory must have been very difficult for him!

Despite the falling standards he was head teacher from 1869 to 1892 and actually died whilst still in post on 28th February 1892 (Trust minute book).

Mr Ovendon is appointed to replace Mr. Sutton and more or less immediately the attendance and the standards improve. He appears to have raised the attendance figures by offering a prize to those with full attendance records.

1895 "School considered to be one of the best in the district. 114 on roll".[14]

In three years he appears to have turned the school around.

Attendance

Both the head teacher's salary and any grants to the school were affected by the attendance figures. Attendance did not become compulsory until 1880. Therefore the head would often have to work hard to keep the children coming to school even after it had become compulsory.

In a country village such as Colton, many reasons would often stop children attending and the school log books are full of the reasons why they do not come.

1870 "Only 24 present the rest absent on various work such as threshing, cow and pig tending, nursing younger children, minding the house etc".

Some reasons for absenteeism abstracted from the School log book in the 19th Century are–

Collecting the harvest.
1873 "Many older children absent in the hayfields".
Potato picking.
1870 "Many still away potato and acorn picking".
Bird scaring.1866
"Most of those absent scaring birds returned to school".

Local Fairs

1874 "Rugeley horse fair prevented many who had to come from that direction being here owing to the number of horses on the road".

Bad Weather

This is constantly being recorded in the log books right from the beginning. Children often did not turn up because there were floods or deep snow and on many occasions the school had to close.

"School closed on account of deep floods. Water is up to the school wall".

"A terrific blizzard started this afternoon. …The blizzard raged on and off from Friday to Monday morning. The snow is about 3ft. deep. Even milk cannot be fetched from farms… On Monday not a single child turned up for school".

Illness and Infections

There were epidemics of illnesses such as measles, whooping cough and scarlet fever that closed the school down for three or four weeks at a time.

1895 "School closed for another two weeks on account of a measles epidemic. The school is being thoroughly cleaned. The old well is closed up and a new one has been sunk".

1912. There were many not attending because the nurse had excluded them because they "had itch and body lice".

In the 1894 when the children were receiving prizes for good attendance, the keen photographic eye of Frederic Bonney of Colton House and a Trustee of the school photographed some of these children outside the school. We are also fortunate enough to know who they are from an entry in the log book.

Photo by Frederic Bonney.

The children's names were Edward Sharratt, Georgina Nicklin, Annie Tooth, Harry Upton, Alice and John Allsopp, Joseph Glenn, William Devalle, Charles Cooper, Emmie Norman, Edward Upton, and Herbert Edward. Some of these family names are still be recognisable in Colton today.

Celebrations

The children were also involved in lots of celebrations in this period, one of the biggest being the May Day celebrations. From the photographs, again courtesy of Frederic Bonney; most people in the village seem to have been involved and particularly the children. Bonney has left a legacy of lots of photographs of the May Day celebrations particularly of the May Queen who is always a schoolgirl.

There were also parties and teas however. There are a number of log book entries that record tea on the lawns of either Bellamour Hall where Mr. Horsfall lived or at Bellamour Lodge.

It is Frederic Bonney we have to thank for taking a picture of the infant school children and their teacher Miss Mansell in 1898.

This has provided us with a lasting record of a group of children who lived in the village then.

Miss Mansell

We know something of Miss Mansell from the Trustees Minute Book.

She was appointed as an assistant teacher to help teach the infants in 1895. She had previously been teaching at the Edgmond National (Church of England) school near Newport and had served her apprenticeship in a girl's school in Newport. She had passed her first year examination papers in 1892. She lodged with the village blacksmith and his family.

Miss Mansell and her class, photo by Frederic Bonney.

We therefore have a remarkable snapshot not only by the camera but also from a written record of someone who taught at Colton in the late 19th Century.

She left the school upon her marriage. At this time female teachers could not teach once they had married!

Scales of Pay in the early years.

Again from the Trustees minute Book and from receipts kept with the school logs we know that in–

1873 Mr. Sutton, Headteacher was paid £50.00.

1903 Mr. Ovenden, Headteacher was paid £142.00. per annum including superannuation. He had to pay rent for

Elm Cottage and at that time it was paid to Mr. Horsfall who owned the house.

The Assistant Teachers like Miss Mansell were paid £55.00 per annum.

The Pupil Teachers were paid £12. 00 per annum.

In 1898 there appear to have been five teachers at the school as well as the head; Miss Garner, Miss Mansell, Miss Yates, B. Stevenson and Edward Sharratt.

Looking at the pay they were receiving it would appear that Miss Mansell was the only one with qualifications.

What did the early school look like?

When the school was first built it was a lot smaller than the school you see today. There was no playing field or garden attached. These all were added later. If you look at a picture of the school just at this time, you will see there were only two classrooms and a porch. The classroom at the back, the north classroom, was where Miss Garner taught the infants. This room had a "gallery" - a raised tiered area for desks so that the teacher could see all the children sitting in rows at one glance. This is where the pupil teacher would also watch over the children and help to instruct them. It would all have been very formal!

The main classroom at the front was sixty feet long and divided by a partition. The rooms were heated by a coal stove. It must have been dark in this room because fairly soon after it is built, two more windows were put in at the front.

The toilets were earth closets at the back of the school. There was no running water.

As numbers grew, in 1894 a new classroom was added to the right hand side of the entrance. In 1920 a garden was added and gardening became a subject on the curriculum.

In 1925 central heating replaced the open fire grates in the large classroom and the coal stove in the infant room. Just think of what health and safety would think of that today!!

The gallery in the infant classroom was removed.

In 1931 electricity was installed. In 1936 Water was installed.

The First World War

Again from the school log books we hear how the First World War affected the school.

1914

"The elder children are now leaving school as soon as they can get away. There is a great demand for domestic servants and the girls are spoken for long before they are 13 years of age. The boys are wanted on the farms because so many have enlisted in the war".

1914

"Some pupils absent as they have been guarding railway bridges all night. They were boy scouts".

1916

"School children allowed outside to see a regiment of soldiers march past".

1917

"The children have subscribed 16/- towards comforts for the wounded soldiers at Ravenhill hospital. More than a ton of chestnuts has been gathered by the children…" It is believed that these were dried and the shells were used in the manufacturing of gas mask filters.

1917

"School closed by the direction of the education committee to celebrate the breaking of the German line by the Staffordshire Regiments".

Reorganisation

Until 1930 the children of the village received their secondary education at Colton unless they were very bright and passed a scholarship. If they passed and their parents could afford to let them go, the boys would go to Rugeley Grammar school and the girls would go to Stafford High school for Girls. This often involved some hardship for parents because all uniform and school books had to be paid for.

In 1930 Staffordshire Education Authority decided to re-organise secondary education in this area. They decided to make a central secondary school at Colwich whilst schools such as Colton, Hixon, Blithfield and Great Hayward became primary schools.

Until after the war all children at the age of 11 transferred to Colwich unless they passed a scholarship to go to Rugeley Grammar School or Stafford Girls High. Those who went to Colwich left at 13.

Second World War

Like many country villages in England in the Second World War, the villagers played host to a group of evacuees. Colton received a group of children from Westgate on Sea on the south coast.

This is a picture of Tony Atkinson and his sister being seen off by their mother before he boarded the train that would bring them to Staffordshire. Tony got in touch with the History Society in 2005 and at the Exhibition of that year we were able to reunite him with some of the friends he made in Colton during that time and some other evacuees who had also been in the village.

The head teacher during this period was Mr. Broughton and a number of present day villagers, as well as the evacuees, remember him vividly.

Again there are lots of entries in the school log books concerning this period.

Jan. 1940. "Soldiers billeted at Colton House helped to clear the snow off the railway. Colton road was impassable to traffic for 10 days until it was cleared by the soldiers. Snow was piled 6ft. deep on each side. …There was a shortage of coal, food was scarce, especially meat. Potatoes became unobtainable for farmers would not open their clamps. School did not reopen until 12th February".

After the War

1953 school meals provided by the L.E.A. commenced for those children travelling some distance to school.

1954 Due to rising costs the Trust was finding it increasingly difficult to run the school and therefore applied for help from the Diocese.

1954 The school becomes grant aided by Lichfield Diocese.

1955 The "Barchester Scheme", a fund of money held by the Diocese, helps aid Colton school.

1963 In order to raise some money the Trust sell Webb's Cottages for £1,250. They are pulled down and new houses are erected on the site.

Change of Head Teacher

In 1959 Mr. Broughton who had been appointed in 1923 and was the longest serving head in the history of the school; retired after 36 years. An advert was placed in order to find a new head and this is what the Trustees requested .

Qualities required for appointment to the Headship, 1959:
"Good churchman.
Rural background– almost essential.
Age group 35-40 preferred.
Family background–domestic harmony.
Sympathetic wife, man with children. Personality speech free from pronounced alien dialect, morally sound.
Residence in village essential".

Just imagine trying to get away with an advert like that today!! [15]

Changes to the School from 1959 to the present

1959 The new head Mr. Waters introduces a school uniform. He and the rector of the time also decided to change the name from Colton United School to Colton St. Mary's School, to acknowledge the fact that it is now an Church Aided school.

The Trustees became anxious about the building and investigated the possibility of building a new school. This idea was finally abandoned in 1964 because of cost but a scheme for modernisation was proposed instead.

1966 Modernisation of the school began and the children were bussed temporarily to Colwich school.

September 1967 the school reopened in the newly extended and refurbished premises.

Head Teachers through the years.

First Head we do not know.

1834 Mr. Simpson. First head we have recorded.

1851 Mr. Lenton

1862 Mr. Dodge

1869 Mr. Sutton

1892 Mr. Ovenden

1915 Mr. Shuttleworth

1923 Mr. Broughton

1959 Mr. Waters

1964 Mr. Mcdowall

1973 Mrs. Hiesley

1983 Mrs. Armitage

1991 Mrs. Evans

1995 Mrs Horden

Mrs. Lavender– head at the end of the century.

The School in recent years

The Trust has had to sell off the property and most of the land it owned to keep abreast of running costs.

The school reached its peak for numbers on roll in 1976 with 121 children attending. However like many village schools it has struggled to maintain viable numbers since then and twice has been under threat of closure. Fortunately for the village the school is still open.

It is still run partly by the Trust.

From the first Free School through to the present day school, it has been an essential part of Colton village life.

Notes

1-7.   School Trust Papers

8-9.   School Log Book

9-10   Trust papers

12.   Log Book

13-14. Trust Papers

Chapter Ten

The 20th Century

The 20th Century

On writing this final chapter we have relied particularly upon recollections of people living in the village. We have also relied heavily for the first half of the century on the school log books that the head of the school was required to keep.[1] The log books recorded events that affected the school and the village almost on a daily basis. For our other source, for the second half of the century, we have extracted information from newspaper articles printed in the local papers and fortunately kept by two or three of the villagers.[2] Despite Colton appearing to be a quiet village backwater in this century, it had its moments of controversy and drama. Many of these were recorded in the local newspapers of the times such as the Rugeley Mercury, the Rugeley Times, the Rugeley Post and the Staffordshire Advertiser. There was a mass of material available but our choice, we hope, reflects the changes that were going on both nationally and in the village itself and gives a flavour of life in Colton.

Poster courtesy of Staffs. County Council Educ. Dept.(3)

The new century effectively started with the death of Queen Victoria in 1901 and the coronation of the new King Edward VII in 1902. Colton celebrated the coronation with a day of festivities around the village. Mrs. Horsfall, who had remained living at Bellamour Hall after her husband's death, kindly sponsored some of the activities. The day reflected the fact that at the beginning of this century life remained very much as it had always been in Colton. Colton was still in the hands of particular landowners, the Horsfall family at Bellamour, the Bagots owners of Little Hay Manor Farm, the Whitgreaves, owners of Boughey Hall Farm and the Bonney family descendents of the Peggs and the Smiths. However their influence on decisions affecting the life of the parishioners had by now begun to wain considerably.

In 1894 the Parish Council Act had been passed. Local Parish Councils were created all over the country where elected members now became the people who made the important decisions on parish matters. The clerkship of Colton parish stayed for 65 years in the hands of one Colton family. John Upton held the position, along with the position of Overseer for the Poor Rate, for 11 years. He was followed by his son Ernest although in 1926 he lost the role of Overseer of the Poor Rate when it was assumed by the Rural District Council. The

Cecil Ravenscroft on becoming an articled clerk. He became Colton's parish clerk.

Clerkship then passed to Cecil Ravenscroft, grandson of John Upton.

The photograph of Cecil Ravenscroft is courtesy of his daughters and shows him receiving his award upon becoming an articled clerk. It is Cecil that we have to thank for saving copies of the many articles that appeared in the local papers and now provide us with a huge resource.

Despite their declining influence, The Horsfalls were still a major employer, employing staff in both the house and on the estate. The head of the household, Henry Leeke Horsfall, was still styled "Lord of the manor of Colton" by Whites directory of the County of Staffordshire.[4]

Picture taken outside Bellamour Hall. Courtesy Express & Star.

The population of Colton at the 1901 Census was recorded as 760 and the largest amount of those in employment worked on the land or associated trades such as blacksmith or wheelwright. This accounted for 32.5%[5] of the workforce. 21.5%[6] of those in work were women, nearly all of them in service jobs such as cook or parlour maid. They worked in all of the large houses in the neighbourhood. The railway had brought some new jobs and provided work for 31 men in 1901.[7]

This coming century was soon to witness a huge change in employment and lifestyles. The social structure, the types and nature of employment, mobility and communications, even our diets were going to be completely different at the end of the century from how they had been at the beginning. Life in the village as elsewhere was to change beyond all recognition in less than a hundred years.

When we interviewed two of the oldest residents of the village for this book, they described their early life at the beginning of this century. 97 year old Sam Jones and his sister Lil Redmand, described their early life in their home at Stockwell Heath. "We lived in a cottage where there was no running water; piped water didn't come into the village until the 1930's. We shared a well with the cottage next door. There was no electricity, that didn't come into the village until the 1930's either. People grew their own vegetables in the back garden and we, like lots of people in the village, had some chickens and some pigs. Nobody starved but there wasn't any money for luxuries. Our entertainment was playing in the fields around the village or on hot days swimming in the brook in the deep water by Bloors Meadow. School was down in the village. You went there until you were 14 and then you left to go to work. What the Headteacher and the Rector said was law. You did not dare argue. Sundays you went first to church and then to Sunday School where Miss Rotchell was the teacher until 1957. Miss Rotchell lived in Lucy Berry Cottage. If it was a nice day she would take you for a walk afterwards. Transport was your own two feet or if you were very lucky a ride in a horse and trap. The Upton family who lived down in the High House had a horse and trap. They had a shop there and Mrs Williscroft also used to have a little general store in her cottage opposite. She moved over the road to Cyprus Cottage in 1913 and opened her shop up there. Her daughter took it over and had it for a long time (until the late 1960's). Charlie Dilly used to bring bread and groceries in a horse drawn wagon twice a week from the Co-op in Rugeley. In the 1940's the Co-op purchased a van and Charlie used to drive this into the village with the groceries."

Charlie Dilley and his horse drawn bread van.

"There was a lock up butcher's shop in front of the Greyhound pub that used to open on Tuesday and Friday afternoons."

*Butchers in front of the Greyhound
probably in the early 1920's.*

The major event that triggered off the process of dramatic change in this century was the First World War. For the first time ever virtually every household in this country was affected in some way. Sam Jones was still a small boy when the First World War broke out and so he remained at home in Colton but other young men from Colton were old enough to fight. A number of them went to fight in the trenches of France and Belgium and 17 of them did not return. Their names are perpetuated on the village war memorial and also in the book "Of those Who Lie in Foreign Fields", researched and written by a past resident of Colton, Squadron Leader R. L. Stanley MBE.[8] In his book he records something about all these young men and where they lost their lives. Thomas Key for instance, who had lived with his parents in

High Street Colton, lost his life on a battlefield in France in November 1916 at the age of 19.

The school log book records how children from the village helped the war effort, "the elder children are now leaving school as soon as they can get away. There is a great demand for domestic servants and the girls are spoken for long before they are 13. The boys are wanted on the farms as many men have enlisted for the war". (Jan 1914) "The children have subscribed 16 shillings towards comforts for the wounded soldiers at Ravenhill hospital" (Oct 1917).

The Inter-War Years

The high death toll in Colton was replicated in communities all over the country, something that had never happened before. This had a tremendous impact on attitudes towards those who were considered to be running the country and "in control" of our lives. Up until this war Britain had been a deferential society but the First World War was the beginning of its death knell. The industrialization of the previous century, coupled with the development of education for all, had brought about increased political awareness and activity amongst working men. When women obtained the vote in the 1920's the whole population became enfranchised for the first time. These factors all contributed to changes in our society. Opportunities opened up that had never been available before to most of the population. Working people began to make their voices heard in a way that they had never been able to in the past.

At the same time many of the large estates and manors that had formed the backbone of the British way of life for centuries began to break up. Many of their owners could no longer afford the running costs with rising wages and the increased costs of living. This was exacerbated when death duties increased dramatically after the first war. At the death of Mrs. Horsfall the Bellamour Estate was split up into lots and sold by her stepson on the 4th June 1921. All the furniture from the house was sold off and the house was soon pulled down because it was too costly to run. The "Manor of Colton" that had been in existence for over 900 years and had shaped the lives of most of the people living in Colton through the centuries, ceased to be. The remains of the house that you see there today are those of the first Bellamour Hall built in the 17th Century. Nothing remains of the second hall.

Likewise in 1921 the Whitgreave estates were broken up and sold and after 400 years of ownership by this family, a very much smaller Boughey Hall Farm passed into new ownership, most of its land having been sold off separately.

Little Hay Manor farm lasted a little while longer. It too soon went the way of the others on the death of Lord Bagot in 1932 when his successor had to sell the Bagot Estates to cover the death duties incurred. Manor Farm was bought by the sitting tenants, the Mellor family, who had been there since the 1919.

In the inter-war years some of the men in the village still obtained employment as farm labourers on the local farms such as Manor Farm.

Many however now found employment elsewhere. They were employed in the tanyard in Rugeley, at Henry Blunn's tin factory by the Trent Valley station where they made tin trunks, the Derby Oxide Colour Works also by the station, and at the goods yard at the station. Those who worked at the tannery could be distinguished by the smell on their clothes and those who worked at the Oxide works by the red pigment on their clothes and skin!

Workers at Manor Farm

As the century progressed an increasing number found employment slightly further afield in places like the mines at Cannock and Brereton. Everyone had to walk to work and those going to Rugeley used the path from Colton across the fields that came out by Fog Cottages. This path had been improved at the beginning of the century by the Rev. Parker. He had paid for the laying down of blue bricks and the erecting of iron gates and turnstiles that are still there today. He also had the four Martlin Cottages built to provide accommodation for four Colton families at a reasonable rent. In 1938 the cottage nearest the Martlin field became the village post office, where it remained until the 1960's.

Another factor that became fundamental to change in this century was the development of the motor vehicle and its increased availability to the general public, although it was not until after the Second World War that this availability gained momentum. Up until the Second World War vehicles were few and far between in the village. In the 1920's beer was being delivered to the Greyhound Pub by a lorry from the breweries at Burton.[9] This was an 8hp Achilles car. Mr. Broughton the headteacher at Colton School was one of the first people in the village to acquire a car, shortly followed by Mr. Cooper another local resident. The other person who came regularly into the village in a car would be the doctor.

A picture of an early car outside the Dun Cow.
Its registration shows that it was only the 84th
registered in Staffordshire.

The School Log Book records another new form of transport flying over Colton village in July 1930, causing a real stir. This was the R 100 airship. "Most of the children got up at 6.00 a.m. in the morning to see it," (School Log, July 1930.)

The Second World War brought more mechanisation to the village in the form of tractors to work the fields in the absence of men who were away fighting. The farms had to become mechanised quickly and farmers were helped by the aid of a scheme whereby they could lease tractors. Manor Farm had tractors under this scheme.

The sense of a close knit community in Colton remained very strong for the first half of the century with the church still providing a focus for much of village life and activities. Some organisations were started and flourished in this period. The Mothers Union started just before the First War, lapsed and then was revived again in 1941 by the wife of the Rector.

The W. I. started in 1937 and still continues today.

Photo of WI members in 1963

For a few years in the 1920's and 30's there was an active Girl Guide troop.

The village had a football team from before the First War. They used to play on the Martlin Hill and called themselves 'Colton St. Mary's'. During the Second War they regularly held matches between themselves and prisoners, usually Italian, from the prisoner of war camps situated near Rugeley. This team eventually disbanded due to a lack of young men.

The football team of 1912

The War Years

When war was declared in 1939 Colton as everywhere else was ordered to take precautionary measures. Blackout material was purchased to black out all sorts of lighting. Air raid wardens and billeting officers were appointed amongst the villagers and gas masks were issued to everyone. Older villagers remember how their horrible pig snout appearance and disinfectant and rubber odour made the danger seem all the more real to everybody. Every household received a pamphlet "How to protect your home against air raids". Fortunately this was never necessary in Colton because it was not in the direct line of fire for bombing raids. However on 25th November 1940, 12 delayed action bombs did fall in the Parish. Six fell in Wilmour Farm fields one in Lount Farm fields, one near the church and the others around Martlin fields and

Martlin Hill. Those that fell around the Martlin disappeared in the running sandy soil never to be discovered. This caused quite a stir with the village boys hunting for trophies![10]

Soon young men from the village were called up to go and fight. In this war only one young man from the village unfortunately lost his life.

Rationing of food was soon introduced and continued until 1954. Most people in Colton grew their own vegetables and had some access to extra meat other than on ration, although it was very limited. The headmaster at the school had all the boys growing vegetables in the school garden. The Head frequently recorded this activity in the log book.

Early in the war a squad of Royal Engineers was billeted at Colton House and they helped to clear the 3 feet of snow from the Colton Road in the bad winter of 1940. The road had been impassable for ten days.

Sam Jones remembers still the very bad winter of 1941 when his pregnant wife urgently needed a midwife. Due to the

The snow of 1940

heavy snowfalls the Colton Road was blocked and he had to ask for the services of a local farmer to fetch the midwife in his horse and cart. In those days you did not have the advantage of a telephone!

In June 1940, 49 evacuees and their teachers from St. Saviours Church of England School in Westgate on Sea in Kent came to Colton. This bewildered little group each member with a label, gas mask and small case was "chosen by women from the village for accommodation. The Colton school children were intrigued by the fact that we had come so far whereas we evacuees were horrified by the sanitation in the village. The water was still coming from pumps and it was so dark at night time!" (Recollections of Tony Atkinson an evacuee in Colton in the war).

The class at St. Saviour's Westgate on Sea before
they were sent to Colton.

By 1944 some American soldiers were billeted at Colton House and provided a great source of fascination. They came to dances that were held at the Reading Room. Some black American soldiers were based at Admaston and villagers remember one truck bouncing off the parapet of the bridge and then somersaulting, seriously hurting a couple of the soldiers. Harry Secombe, a famous performer, was stationed in the camp established in the grounds where Bellamour Hall had once stood.

The end of the war was celebrated with the school closing for the day and a tea being provided by Mrs. Morley on the lawn of Bellamour Lodge for the village children.[11]

Post-War Britain

The war had ended but new problems arose after the initial euphoria of the victory. The period from VE Day in 1945 to the birth of the Welfare State in July 1948 was a time of great austerity and dramatic change and major economic and social reforms. There was also the threat from Russia of a phoney war which was marked by military and nuclear tension between Western Alliances and the Soviet Union. The British Empire was increasingly unsure of itself. The economy became reliant upon American loans and the need to feed a starving Europe ensured that domestic rationing almost as big a burden to the ordinary person than it was during the war. Colton however coped well with this problem, being a farming community villagers soon found ways of supplementing their rations. Austerity became a way of life to children of the war years and this they had ingrained into them, to the extent that even now in the 21st century these particular adults hate waste of any sort. Clothing coupons were also necessary for almost every item of clothing and this form of rationing did not end until February 1st 1949. With the removal of this restriction the ladies of the village had the freedom to try out the new fashions that were being quickly introduced. When sweet rationing finally ended as late as 1953, children had the wonder of going into a sweet shop to buy any sweet they wanted. Children who had grown up during the war had only been able to previously buy cough sweets.

Teenagers did not have much materially but had a freedom unknown to today's children, that of personal safety.

Looking back over these years it was amazing how everyone must have pulled together, putting all petty grievances aside in the desperate struggle for the survival of Britain and freedom and our way of life.

Identity cards and ration books that everybody had to use.

A Very Cold Winter

In 1947 the country experienced one of the coldest winters on record and older villagers could remember snow piled halfway up the houses. The snow began to fall in early January and it snowed and snowed with an easterly wind causing heavy drifting, continuing until late spring. Many of the schoolchildren were unable to get to school for days on end. Delivery into the village was extremely difficult especially along the Colton Road into Rugeley. Snow was as high as the hedges and the canals were all frozen solid.

November 1947
A Fairytale in a Grey world

The gloom of the post war years was lifted briefly when it was announced that Princess Elizabeth was to be married to Philip Mountbatten, whose father was Prince Andrew of Greece. The wedding took place in Westminster Abbey in November 1947.

The Creation of the
National Health Service

Free medical care for everyone was passed by the government after difficult negotiations between Aneurin Bevan (Health Minister) and doctors. This was a great relief to the average villager as it meant no more huge bills to pay if anyone was ill. Villagers had until then paid into what was called an "Oddfellows Club", which meant that they could pay by saving small amounts weekly for doctor's bills. There had never been a resident doctor in Colton and villagers had to travel to Rugeley. However, doctors made visits to people in their own homes when necessary.

Nationalisation

A major programme of nationalisation was undertaken in 1948. This would have had an impact on many villagers because they worked in the local coal mines, on the railways and in the electricity industry all of which were nationalised. In basic terms nationalisation meant the purchase of private industries and businesses by the state so that they could provide for the national good or so it was claimed by the politicians who introduced it. On the whole this resulted in providing much better working conditions in all of these industries together with promised pensions.

The B.B.C. produced a programme called "New Lamps for Old" which featured many local miners including a few from Colton. In the programme they explained that they felt the comradeship in the Brereton colliery was better than in any other and stated that even in bad times Brereton colliery, otherwise named "Mr. Cadman's Pit", always worked regularly. During interludes in the programme, much of which was recorded in the Talbot Inn in Rugeley, humour and song of the miners could be heard in the background. The number of men employed in this pit was gradually reduced from 1,500 to 250 men at the closure. Brereton was closed down on July 1st 1960. Lea Hall colliery in Rugeley then became the nearest mine.

Three deputies and an acting overman with 120 years underground experience at Brereton chat with acting manager Mr. J. R. Price at the end of the day shift. They are (left to right) H. Perrins, P. Bradshaw, M. Cooper and D. Myatt.

1951 Festival of Britain

The gloom in Britain was effectively lifted for a short while by this great Festival. It was an immediate success with people from all over Britain flocking to see the exhibition in London. A "Skylon" which was erected in the festival site was a large vertical feature symbolizing the spirit of hope in the country.

The Festival's new architectural style was very influential and changed the public's taste for new design permanently. This was soon reflected in the style of houses and furniture in particular. Colton had many dilapidated old cottages and gradually new style houses were built to replace them.

Coronation Day in Colton

The coronation of Elizabeth II was held on 2nd June 1953. This was a sumptuous affair marking the end of the austerity years although it was cold and it rained throughout the coronation day itself. Many people around the country bought their very first television so that they could watch the ceremony and the first pictures of the Queen on television created much excitement. The whole country was on the edge of the new Elizabethan age. The day was also enhanced when the news was released that a British team had become the first to conquer Everest.

In Colton the preparations for celebrating began some months before the event. The seven members of the Parish Council divided the Parish between them. They visited each household to collect contributions towards the costs of the day.

On the Sunday previous to Coronation Day (which was Wednesday) there was a special service of Evensong at 6.30p.m. in Colton church. The church was decorated with red, white and blue flowers. Many people attended this service. As Coronation Day dawned there was a service of Holy Communion at 8.15 a.m. in the church. In the middle of the morning there was a well attended open air service held in front of the War Memorial. Then everyone went home to watch the Coronation service on the television if they were lucky enough to have one or to listen to it on the radio if they hadn't.

During the afternoon a team of people prepared cold meat and a salad type meal in the Reading Room (village hall). From late afternoon until early evening parishioners arrived to partake of this meal. There were several sittings to accommodate everyone from the Parish. Every child, including the under-fives and all who were in full time education, received a Coronation mug.

Following the meal in the Reading Room, everyone who could, climbed to the top of the Martlin hill to witness a mammoth bonfire. After this many returned to the Reading Room to enjoy dancing.

The total cost of the celebrations was £261.14s.6½d. On 5th February 1954 a public meeting was held to dispose of a surplus of £62.0s.9d left over from the Coronation Day celebrations. The following suggestions were adopted. A golden privet hedge to be planted behind the war memorial. A Burma oak seat with brass plate coronation inscription to be installed on the Pinfold. A new electrically heated copper (water heater) and 15 new chairs to be purchased for the Reading room. The surplus money was to be handed over to the management committee of the Reading Room on the express understanding that it be earmarked for improving the ladies toilet. Also purchased were wine glasses for the Women's Institute although these were to be used for other occasions apart from W.I. events. Also 5 or 6 mugs were to be given to children who had been born shortly after Coronation Day.

Colton Post Office and Post Ladies

Residents of Colton made a presentation in July 1956 to Miss Rotchell who had been village post lady for 42 years. It was stated that Miss Rotchell had walked 180,000 miles delivering letters.

Following her resignation Mrs. Vera Collins delivered the post and after her Mrs. Blanche Ravenscroft, a well known character in the village. She took over the job as post lady riding her bicycle around the village. After 10 years as a temporary, she started work for the Post Office on a regular basis. However, Mrs. Ravenscroft was much more than just the "Village Post Lady". She delivered messages and notes from one villager to another. She also welcomed new families into the village encouraging them to join in all village activities. If on her post round she noticed curtains were not opened there would be a friendly knock on the door to see if anyone was ill or to remind people that it was time for work! Her pet hates were, blizzards, naughty schoolboys who loosed her tyres down and villagers who sent home kippers for their friends through the post from their holidays! Upon the sad death of Mrs. Ravenscroft whilst she was delivering the post, Mrs. Rose Deval took over. She was in fact the last Colton resident to act as post lady. After that it was delivered by van from Rugeley.

Colton Post Office had been situated at No.1. Martlin Cottages. However after 38 years Mrs Constance Deacon, who had been sub-postmistress for 26 years, retired.

The post office moved to The Cottage Stores situated at the top of the village (High Street) and owned by Mr. & Mrs. Jack Brown.

Miss Rotchell delivering the post

Inside 'Cottage Stores'

After the closure of this shop in the 1970's, the Post Office continued to operate for a while in the kitchen of Mrs. Ruth Jones' house situated in High Street.

The only shop then left in the village was the general store situated in the High House and run by Mrs. Upton. After Mrs. Upton died suddenly in her shop one day, Mrs Ruth

Jones took over this shop and incorporated the Post Office. The shop continued to function here under different owners but as more villagers acquired motor cars and could shop further afield, the death knell of the village shop was heard as in so many other villages around the country.

Vegetable Show 1944

A vegetable show which was held on Saturday 16th September 1944 was probably a pre-cursor to the Produce Guild formed in 1957. The entire village turned out to this Grand Vegetable and Agricultural Produce Show. It raised more that £100 to send "Comforts to Young men and girls from Colton who have joined the Fighting Forces in recognition of the services they are rendering to us". Obviously by September 1944 the villagers were in no doubt about a quick finish to the war, stating that "We are hopeful that the recent success achieved by the members of all services will make this perhaps the last appeal before the enemy is finally defeated. The committee trust that you will by your generous support make this occasion an "A BIG THANK YOU" to our service friends".

Colton Produce Guild

A Public Meeting was held on March 1st 1957 in the village hall where a talk was arranged for the County Chairman to set

out the advantages of starting such a Produce Guild i.e. new social contacts, added interest in village life, help in the garden from well known speakers and also cheaper buying of seeds, fertilizers and lime etc. due to bulk buying.

Following on from this talk it was agreed by villagers to start a Colton Produce Guild.

The first committee was formed with a Chairman, Mr. R. Brundle, Secretary and Treasurer and a committee of seven members. Miss Dorothy Jones was appointed Secretary and continued in this post until she died aged over ninety.

The Produce Guild is one of the very successful clubs to have been formed in the 20th Century in Colton and provides a now much needed opportunity for parishioners to meet socially.

"It has always had a very varied and interesting calendar. This starts with a Christmas Social in January which takes the form of a party with food and home grown entertainment. This can include anything from a pantomime to a variety show produced by members. For many years the programme would not be complete without a monologue by a long standing and much loved member Nev. James who has lived in the village nearly all his life. This entertainment together with Jack Brown's home made wine, makes for a wonderful evening. Members of other Staffordshire guilds are also invited. A meeting is held every month with varied speakers mainly on gardening and other related subjects. An Annual General meeting is held in April when a new committee is elected. There is a Rose Show in July. There is a whole day coach outing in the summer to various gardens with favourites being trips to villages with open gardens, usually somewhere in the Cotswolds. The Annual Fruit, Flower and Vegetable Show which takes place in September is always very well received with members competing with their garden produce and the ladies showing off their cooking skills as well as flower arranging and craft work. After the judging the show is open to visitors and the village hall is always packed with a wonderful genial atmosphere abounding. In October the Guild has its Harvest Supper when members produce a superb home grown meal with wonderful home made fruit pies.

After 50 years of continuous meetings the Produce Guild is as strong as ever at encouraging a close knit community".

Rowdyism in Colton

In 1959 villagers protested that there was an urgent need for a youth club in the village, as youngsters had nothing to occupy them. This caused problems as they were often standing around making a lot of noise.

Lack of a police patrol was evident in Colton when practically every other village in the area had a patrol. This has been a regularly recurring theme in Colton as successive generations of youngsters have hung around in groups somewhere in the village because they 'have nothing to do,' Will it ever be any different!

Youth Club

Various attempts have been made to occupy the youngsters in the village over this period. The headmaster of the school ran a youth club for a while in the 1960's. Since then there

have been several attempts to run a youth club in the village. The Parish Council and Village Hall committee had both actively started clubs and given funds but the stumbling block in recent years had always been youth club leaders. Youths of the village have a wonderful amenity in the village hall field as it gives them a large common open space if they can find someone suitable to run a club.

Colton Football Team

As mentioned earlier there has been a Football team in Colton since the beginning of the century. Over the years several parents in the village started football teams for teenagers. During the 1980's a new team was formed called The Colton Swifts football team. Unfortunately there appeared to be no level pitch on Colton ground so their training had to be done elsewhere. This continued for many years before the team finally disbanded although one tradition has been retained from the early years, that of the annual Boxing Day match between the Married and Single men.

Colton to Have New Lights
2nd April 1954

Colton villagers no longer had to grope their way along the main street after dark. Public lighting which had been controversial for some years was now installed. The re-siting of one of the lights and the provision of yet another meant, however, that the subject had not entirely disappeared from the Parish Council agenda.

The meeting in the Reading room was overwhelmingly in favour of nine new street lights to be installed around the village. Estimates of the cost caused a certain amount of controversy. The M.E.B. stated that while it was possible to arrange for the street lights to be extinguished during moonlit nights the capital charges which would have to be included in the hire charges would more than off-set the saving in the electric consumed. The approximate cost of the parish rate would be 4½ pence for 6 lights 2½ pence for three lights and two lights 1½ pence. Some councillors asked for a modification of the number of lights. However one person asked if the proponents of the modified scheme involved would be willing to provide torches for the old age villagers! It was also stated that villagers must expect that rates would have to be increased to meet the cost of lights.

More New Houses For Colton

By 1959 development had been going on steadily at the upper end of High Street with new houses known as Fair Meadows being built. Also in Heath Way a number of rural type council houses had been built. Before this time Colton had been largely a village of old houses which had been allowed to get into a state of decay. Many of these houses were stated by the council to be unfit for habitation and were demolished, particularly many of the houses in High Street.

HOUSES COME TO COLTON

A corner of the bar in Colton's ancient inn, the Dun Cow. Standing is Mr. R. Boycott, whose mother is licensee. The picture (right) gives a close-up of the new development that is taking place above High Street.

Old dilapidated cottages in High Street

These were replaced in places with new bungalows and individual homes interspersed with old buildings which still stand to this day.

Mechanisation on the Farm

Mechanisation took a leap forward on a Colton farm with the arrival of a combine harvester at Manor Farm in the 1950's followed by a further one in the 1960's bought by Mr. J. C. Price owner of Bellamour Farm. In an article to the local paper he explained how the grain went through the whole process of harvesting without being touched by hand. The system needed only seven men for a smooth operation. With good weather they could complete 20 acres in a day, much time saving on the old methods of harvesting.

Estate Would Ruin Colton's Rural Beauty Say Villagers

During the 1960's after hearing of a proposal by Lichfield District Council, villagers complained that a proposed building of 250 houses would "literally tear the heart out of the village". The proposal was strongly objected to by villagers, together with the Ministry of Agriculture stating that the land on which the development was to take place was good soil and would be a serious loss not only to the locality but to the nation as a whole. The plan appears to have been subsequently dropped.

Action Urged on Highway Death Trap

Colton's old High Street was long and narrow, meandering uphill from the corner of Bellamour Way and Hollow Lane to the top of the village with new houses being built along the way. However, it had no footpath and no escape for people trapped by traffic between the high banks of the road.

This state of affairs was exacerbated over many years as the traffic gradually increased after the Second World War. The delay was worsened because a sewerage system which had been expected to be started, had not reached fruition. At the Parish Council meeting a member of the Staffordshire Roads and Bridges committee stated that the High Street was one of 279 road improvement schemes not yet programmed. The Parish Council stated that if any child died as a result of this dangerous situation the Roads and Bridges Committee would be held responsible. Owners were willing to dedicate

An impression of the narrow Colton High Street, with banks on each side, which is to be widened and provided with footpaths.

their land for the road widening scheme. Subsequently a successful meeting with county officials was arranged. On 15th January 1972 an urgent road widening scheme was approved. It was going to cost £44,000 and was planned to start later in the year. There would be new footpaths and a drainage system.

Licence Granted for Daily Bus Service to Colton. 1960

The Green Bus Co. was granted a license on January 11th 1960 for a daily bus service. During the 1940's, 50's and 60's the Green Bus Service run by a local company was a vital link for the residents of the village to enable them to shop and do business in Rugeley and further afield. It was a friendly service picking up old people near to their houses giving them a chance to meet with other villagers on their journey.

Train Services

Trent Valley station at Colton had long been a hive of industry with goods being moved, First World War soldiers destined for the training camps on the Chase arriving and departing and later air force personnel in the Second War going to camps at Brindley Heath and Hednesford. This did not last. In the 1960's the government under Dr. Beeching threatened to close Trent Valley Railway station completely but a reduced Stafford to Rugby service was retained. Eventually in 1965 the local passenger and goods service to Walsall was closed. However due to local public pressure some years later a much reduced service to Walsall was re-introduced. Gradually over recent years there has been more investment in the railways and there is now a more efficient local service again.

Flower Festivals

The first flower festival was held in St. Mary's church in 1966. The church was beautifully decorated by the ladies of Colton. There was another festival in 1968. This form of festival died out, being replaced for a while with church flower festivals incorporated into the Village Festivals. There was also one for the Queen's jubilee in 1977. The church has always been beautifully decorated for Christmas, Easter, Whit Sunday and Harvest Festivals.

Old Age Pensioners Committee

Colton Parish Council decided in December 1966 to call a public meeting to consider the formation of a local Old People's Welfare Committee. Several people including the Medical Officer of Health for Lichfield were invited to attend a formation meeting.

Above: The first Flower Festival in 1966

Below: Old Age Pensioners at their formation meeting

COLTON

SHOW: Colton Village Produce
iild and Women's Institute Show
is very successful. The number of

of space): Mrs. T. Preston, Miss
Gwendoline Ravenscroft: black-
currant jam: Mrs. I. R. Brown;
marmalade (three fruit): Mrs. T.
Preston; lemon curd, Mrs. T. Preston
Mrs. Wright, Miss Jones; jelly t

However, the Rector did not think there was any need for "yet another Committee" in Colton, but a villager stated that if a committee were formed he thought it would probably "snowball". A committee was formed and at the first meeting twenty four old people from the Parish attended and were entertained to a tea and social evening. Some said it was the first time that they had ever been invited to anything and all expressed pleasure. A subsequent meeting was arranged with a whist drive and tea. Films were sometimes shown and summer outings arranged. The committee has continued over the years and is still flourishing today with a wonderful Christmas Dinner and entertainment in the village hall and a summer event for the old people every year.

Traction Engine Rallies

For several years starting in 1963 Colton held two-day traction engine rallies in Bellamour Park grounds before moving to the County Showground because it had outgrown the Bellamour site. They were organized by the Colton Village Hall Committee and North Staffordshire and Cheshire Traction Engine Club. They attracted thousands of visitors and large amounts of money were made. Profits were divided equally between the two organisations. The initial funds for Colton were used in 1965 to purchase the field where the present village hall stands. The rally included traction engines, veteran and vintage cars in the main arena with numerous side shows and exhibitions by the North Staffordshire Society of Model Engineers who gave rides on a miniature railway. There was a religious service on Sunday morning. Many Colton parishioners were kept extremely busy acting as stewards for the car parks for the hundreds of cars entering the village.

Traction Engine Rally at Bellamour

Council to Safeguard Ice Age Relics

In March 1974 the council set about saving four Ice Age stones situated at each corner of Brook Bridge. Having been around for 600 million years they were perhaps entitled to be sinking below the surface. They may have been stepping stones at a ford before the bridge was built and then later used to stop cartwheels getting too close to the bridge walls. One of the stones appeared to be missing. After digging around the stone was eventually uncovered and the Council decided to raise the buried stone and clear earth and overgrown grass from around the others.

Should Colton Have House Numbers

In March 1971 the Parish Council decided to ask Lichfield District Council if numbering for houses was now required by law. Houses in half of the village were not numbered. They also asked to discuss the possibility of changing the name of the main street to incorporate "Upper or Lower". The chairman said this was being done to ease the postal services. He said that many houses had particularly difficult names. These could be retained but they would also have to have a number.

Colton Main Road to Have a New Name

In May 1971 the Parish Council agreed that the lower half of the main street was to be called Bellamour Way (previously known as Brook Street) and the upper half High Street.

Tree Planting in Hollow Lane

From 1970 to 1972 discussions took place about planting trees along the bank to stabilize it. There was much discussion as to what types of trees were going to be used to replace these. Eventually it was decided they would be replaced by oak, lime, sycamore and varieties of horse chestnut. These were to have tree preservation orders put upon them.

Best Kept Village Competition

For approximately 20 years Colton entered the Best Kept Village Competition. Finally in 1985 it was won by Colton although the village had been very close on numerous occasions before. The tall plaque commemorating this success was placed opposite to St. Mary's School, catching the eye of everyone approaching the village. Community spirit helped win this trophy, beating 20 other villages from the East/Staffs Lichfield district. Villagers and children helped keep the village clean and tidy throughout the summer, picking up litter, cutting grass verges, pulling out weeds from underneath walls and banks, keeping gardens looking wonderful and taking special care with all public places. The school was

especially praised for encouraging the children to be aware of their environment.

Best Kept Garden Competition

This was a competition organized each year by the Parish Council for every house in the Parish that wished to take part. Various categories were arranged with the Parish Council cup for the best overall flower and vegetable garden, the Richard Morrall cup for the best vegetable garden and the Little Hay rose bowl was awarded for the best flower garden. Supplementary prizes were also awarded to Village Produce Guild members who entered without winning prizes in the Parish Council competition. The annual competition produced a blaze of colour throughout the year. Unfortunately this competition stopped and has not been renewed.

Annual Church Garden Party

The church garden party was an annual event and much looked forward to by parishioners. After twenty five years the annual church garden party was moved in 1967 from a Wednesday fete to a Saturday one. The change was brought about by the move of the August Bank holiday from the beginning to the end of August. The fete was held in the Rectory gardens, and a notable person would open the fete e.g. Lady Bagot.

The money raised was put into the church funds. There would have been a children's fancy dress competition, a treasure hunt, guessing the weight of a cake, clock golf, bowls, giant skittles, a raffle, and numerous side stalls of all types. This had the advantage of bringing together all village people in fellowship and to spare a thought in an enjoyable way for all that the church had brought to everyone over the centuries.

The opening of the 25th garden party

New Rectory for Colton

In the mid 1970's the old rectory was sold and a new rectory was built next to Moreton Brook on the site where the rectory had stood until 1806.

Queen's Silver Jubilee Celebrations

Colton as usual celebrated the event in June 1977 with enthusiasm. It seemed as though the whole village had turned out in the sunshine at Pedley's Croft to absorb the Jubilee spirit. The children entered a Fancy Dress competition with wonderful costumes representing the patriotic theme. Decorated vehicles paraded through the village. A best dressed house competition was judged. Star attraction was a pram race with adults dressed as mothers and babies racing from Stockwell Heath to Colton. This caused much fun with "babies" being catapulted out of prams. There was much evidence of industrious activity in St. Mary's church with villagers exhibiting their local crafts, together with a selection

of bee-keeping by a well known villager, corn dolly exhibition, and a selection of children's paintings and models. A sports day was held on the Monday for the children in the school field. A Jubilee

thanksgiving service was held in the church on Sunday and parties were held for the old age pensioners and the children of the village. A bonfire was lit on the Martlin, a high point in the village although this was not part of an official linking of bonfires throughout the country. Greetings were sent to the Queen on behalf of the people of Colton.

Colton Flower Club

A flower club was formed in the 1980's for the ladies of Colton. There was a meeting in the village hall once a month. There would either be a demonstration by an expert or the ladies produced their own arrangements. Mrs. Gwen Johnson a well known expert flower arranger, who had lived in the village all her life, did the teaching for all the members.

Charles and Diana's Wedding

As with all royal celebrations the whole country joined in the anticipation of joy.

Villagers organized a barn dance in the car park of the Dun Cow public house on the evening of the wedding. Mr. Jack Brown, a well known villager, played music both recorded and live on his accordion and called instructions to the dancers.

A large wedding cake decorated with the names of the Royal couple was the centrepiece of the evening. This was baked by Steven Upton, a young baker from the village, and was enjoyed by all the dancers.

Ever heard of "The Greensleeves," "The Woolybacks" or "The Blue Mountain Band"?

They may not produce hit singles, but Colton folk found their music just as much fun to dance to.

Several villagers organised a barn dance in the car park of the "Dun Cow" as their wedding night celebration.

Mr. Jack Brown played music — both recorded and live on accordion — and called instructions for those uninitiated in barn dancing.

Mr. Brian Bevan had floodlights in the car park so that dancing could continue well into the evening.

A wedding cake, decorated with the names of the Royal couple, was the centrepiece of the feast.

Baked by Steve and Mary Upton, and donated by them and Derek and Vicky Sargeant, the cake was cut by a couple celebrating their 14th wedding anniversary — George and Marion Vernon.

Village Festivals

Colton had had festivals before the Second World War but they had faded out.

In the 1980's the village was desperate to raise money for a new village hall as the old reading room structure was very dilapidated. Various money raising efforts were tried but it was soon realized that the village needed large money

Colton Festival 1936

making efforts to get near to the £85,000 which would be required to build a new village hall. After much discussion there was a feeling among villagers that they would like to organize a Colton Festival. This was to be held in September, a time which coincided with the ancient Market Charter which was given to Colton in medieval times. A public meeting was held in the village hall and a committee was formed. It brought the village together in a way which had not been seen for many years.

It was decided to have market type stalls starting on Pedley's Croft and stretching up the village with stalls on both sides together with exhibitions and many and varied shows.

Villagers opened their gardens, driveways and garages. Everyone in the village started early on Saturday morning and the anticipation grew throughout the day. The village ladies provided lunches and teas in the decorated village hall. For weeks beforehand villagers had been busy making crafts to sell on stalls. One villager made wooden candle holders and cheese dishes from an old yew tree cut down in the churchyard. One of the highlights of the first Festival was a demonstration by Maurice Williscroft, a member of a very old Colton family, who demonstrated his original craft of "Hooping a Wheel". This was done by shrinking an iron rim onto an old fashioned wooden wagon wheel.

Mr. Maurice Williscroft of Forge House, Colton showing children the skills of a wheelwright. Mr. Williscroft's father was a master wheelwright and taught his son the skills but the business had to go over to restoring and making furniture when motor vehicles replaced horses.

Now there are increasing demands for wheelwright skills, Mr. Williscroft can do more of the job he loves best.

After the first year it was decided to hold a festival every two years, and this continued until 1995. Each festival had a theme and villagers dressed in authentic costume, with appropriately dressed villagers guarding Brook Bridge where buying a programme entered you into the village. Themes included a Medieval Festival with everyone wearing beautiful costumes, a European Union theme which represented Britain joining the European Union. At this festival the village was decorated with all the flags of European countries. During this festival on Saturday evening a marquee which had been erected on Pedley's Croft came into use for a German Evening complete with a dance, an Um-Pah band and a bierkeller atmosphere. This was a huge success. This ended the first day of the Festival on a wonderful note. Sunday morning probably started with a few sore heads! However, it nearly always dawned with a beautiful autumn morning, cold with an atmospheric mist drifting across the fields. The morning always started with a church service and then a fun run. Throughout the weekend hundreds of people visited the church which always held a beautiful flower festival, the flower decorations being done by the ladies of the flower club in the theme of the week-end. There were band concerts, keep fit demonstrations, morris men, clog dancers, tug-of-war competitions, men's football matches, model railway exhibitions with art exhibitions in the School, classic car competitions and many more. The whole village was alive and looking very pleased with itself. The money which was made paid for the new village hall which opened in 1992. This was no mean feat for a small village and Colton had excelled itself once again. All the festivals helped to create a great sense of community spirit.

Village Hall Auctions

Auctions of household goods and toys were originally started to raise funds for a new village hall. These auctions, which continue to this day, are enjoyed by both people from outside the village and villagers. While the auction is taking place refreshments are served and these have become well known for their delicious home baked cakes served with tea and coffee. Over the years many people have bid for unusual objects and many people have acquired wonderful bargains, although many of these return at the next auction! The auctions are usually held twice a year, in March and October.

Villagers Battle to Save Post Office
5th September 1991

After fears that the post office was about to close the new owner of the High House reported that he had been granted a new franchise from the post office. He stated that the news came as a boost to the village. For years the village shop had been the centre of village life and a meeting place for villagers. However, due to the expansion of local supermarkets in nearby towns villagers could not afford to pay the price of goods charged by the small shops. This ultimately meant that after a short while Colton's only village shop was forced to close, and one of the main meeting places of the village disappeared. This then left only three notice boards and the Parish Newsletter in which to inform the villagers of events taking place in the village. It was now up to the church and village hall to try to keep the village community together.

End of the Old Village Hall:
In Comes the New Hall

After several years of much fund raising the new village hall was eventually opened by Miss Dorothy Jones, one of the oldest inhabitants of Colton. The opening had been eagerly awaited by villagers as this provided a new hall incorporating a kitchen and toilets.

Many village events have taken place in the new hall, one of the most important being the celebration of the new millennium with a wonderful traditional dinner and dancing late into the first morning of the new century for villagers.

The old village hall (formerly the reading room)

As the church bells rang out to welcome the new millennium villagers could not help but wonder what the new century held in store for the village.

Changes at Colton Church Through This Century

The Rev. Parker, the author of the "History of Colton and the de Wasteneys Family" was the Rector at Colton as the century started. He and his sisters helped the community in many ways. They did not discriminate between those who attended church and those who did not. On one day each week during winter time, families could acquire a large container of stew for their main meal. Every new mother was supplied with a hot dinner for a fortnight. The old men from the Parish were invited to a Christmas meal at the Rectory where food and ale flowed freely. Harriet Parker was an excellent craftswoman in wood and made items for the parish. Her sister Eleanor played the church organ and was choir mistress.

There was a choir of men and boys which declined in the 1920's. A choir was reintroduced in the early 1940's to include girls! Again it declined and then was re-established in 1957 and it sang every Sunday for the next 30 years.

Colton Church Choir

When electricity became available in the village in the 1930's, Maud Oldham paid for its installation in the church in memory of her husband. Other gifts were made during the next 20 years such as the hymn boards, the Mother's Union banner and an electrical organ blower. This was very welcome as the organ had been hand pumped until then. These gifts all had dedications.

The Sunday school flourished during the earlier decades but by the late 1950's it was in decline. It was re-established 13 years later and still flourishes into the 21st century.

The greatest changes in this century were to the church grounds.

In 1957 a new Rector, the Rev. Stanley Towlson, was appointed. It was his vision to open up the view of the church from the road into the village.

Photo showing interior of Colton church with electric lighting

Below: Outside the church as it used to look

The churchyard in an unkempt state.

Land cleared for the new burial ground

He thought that this ancient burial ground could be altered so that mowing by modern machinery could easily be facilitated. This meant that the majority of the gravestones would have to be moved. The Parochial Church Council agreed to this idea and permission was sought from Diocese and granted. First the gravestones were recorded in situ and a plan was made of where they were before they were moved. Where descendents could be traced, permission was sought for the gravestones to be moved. Every family that was approached agreed that this could go ahead.

The project was to be a major change to an area surrounding the village's oldest building and institution. It was therefore not surprising that the project was not without its opponents at the time and many bitter words were exchanged. The Rev. Towlson was given the nickname 'the bulldozer vicar' by some of the parishioners who did not agree with what he was doing. It caused a lot of controversy in the village at the time but the plan, however, went ahead.

Thus began a period of intense activity, much of it being carried out by volunteers from the village who did agree with the plan and who worked hard to carry it out. Soon Pedley's Croft completely changed in appearance. The field edges were pushed back and the mound we see today was created. The hedges, fences, gates and stone wall were removed so that the church could be seen clearly from the road and a flower garden was created on the south side of the church.

In the years that have followed Pedley's Croft has provided a great amenity space for the village and there are fine views of the church as you enter the village.

The men and women who worked on the project are depicted in a window in the church as bees around a hive busy working away.

As the century progressed more changes have occurred inside. New lighting has been installed and overhead electric heaters. In 1977 a new white altar frontal was dedicated in memory of a former churchman. To commemorate an anniversary of a family serving the church and parish, the red altar frontal was completely refurbished in 1996.

As the century drew to a close people were encouraged to join the bell ringing team and this was taken up with enthusiasm. Two new bells were added to the existing ones early in the 21st century.

The Colton Art of Corn Plaiting

This unique art of corn plaiting was introduced to Colton in the 19th Century and continued throughout the 20th

Some of the village ladies who were involved
with the corn plaiting in the early 1930's

Century. The plaits traditionally consisted of wheat, oats and barley. Unfortunately the local production of oats and barley ceased some years ago. The plaits are made by women of the village to adorn the inside of the church around the pillars, font, pulpit and lectern. Before the days of combine harvesters the corn was delivered in sheaths but since the 1950's it has had to be cut by hand.

Traditionally until about 1960 the church was also decorated with holly and ivy woven into long wreaths at Christmas and by box and yew at Easter time. Unfortunately this is one of the age old traditions that has now died out.

Flooding Problems in Colton

Colton has long had problems with the brook breaking its banks and causing flooding by the Brook Bridge. Over the years it has prevented children getting to school and caused problems with vehicles getting in and out of the village. On a number of occasions the New Rectory car park has been flooded. Various attempts were made from the 1980's onwards to try and improve the drainage in that area of the village but it still remains a problem. The village

is surrounded by brooks and in very severe wet weather conditions it is still possible for Colton to be completely cut off. In living memory residents can remember huge amounts of flood water running off the Martlin Hill and the hill behind Manor Farm causing flooding in some houses. Over the years there have been landslides of mud in Hollow Lane. This is now a very topical issue but hopefully flooding will not cause too much of a problem for Colton in the future.

Colton as the 20th Century Ends

At the close of the century Colton in appearance had not changed as much as many villages in the area. There had been some new housing but on nothing like the scale of development that had occurred in some of the other nearby Staffordshire villages.

The significant changes had been to the lifestyles of the people who now lived in the village. At the end of the century most of the people now living here had been born elsewhere and had chosen to come and live in the village. Virtually every household had at least one car and most more than one and nearly all of the working residents now travelled some distance to work. Situated near to many modern amenities and close to major roads, Colton, in the latter years of the century had become a desirable village to live in. However because of the rise in house prices again in the later years of the century, the population of Colton was now made up of far more older people than had ever been the case in previous centuries, because young people could no longer afford the prices of houses in the village. This in turn had created a decline in the number of children attending the village school and the school was forced to seek pupils from further afield in order to stay open. The threat of closure remains ever present.

Fortunately Colton had managed to retain its community spirit and its village atmosphere, two other factors that made Colton a desirable village to live in. The village hall now provided the main focal point for village activities, although the Church was still relatively active and played a part in village life although much diminished compared to previous centuries. The many thriving village organisations have enabled residents to retain the sense of belonging to a community. It is interesting to note that at the end of a century in which so much change had taken place, belonging to a community was, and still is, so important.

Remarkably the population of Colton has fluctuated very little throughout the centuries. In the early Middle Ages it was a big, significant Staffordshire village, now it is a sleepy little village overshadowed by its bigger neighbours. At the end of this century when a Colton resident could be on the other side of the world in a day; could communicate with anyone, anywhere at any time and so many things work at the flick of a switch, one wonders what the scribe who walked through Colton making the first written record of the existence of the village for the Domesday Record, would make of the place now.

Notes

1. School Log Books Courtesy of St. Mary's School Trustees.

2. Press cuttings courtesy of Ruth Williams and Gwen Johnson.

3. 'Colton' Produced by Staffs. County Council Education Dept. Local History Source Book.

4. Whites Directory of 1921 William Salt Library

5. "Occupations in Colton" by Allan Lloyd Colton History society Publication 2006

6. As above.

7. As above.

8. "Of those who lie in Foreign Fields" by R. L. Stanley MBE. & Joy Bratherton. Publ. Anne Loader.

9. 'Colton' as above.

10. Colton and World War II by Jill Croft. Colton History Society Publication 2006.

11. School Log Book as above.

Postscript
Significant Changes to the village
early in the 21st Century

In the millennium year of 2000 mum's of the village decided that it would be nice for the children to have a play area at the rear of the village hall. A committee of mothers was formed and it was decided to apply to the National Lottery fund for a grant. It was found that £43,000 would be needed to build the play area and small garden to the side of the village hall. Much form filling ensued and much to their delight a lottery grant was provided. The play area is extremely well used by all the children of the village, especially as a "letting off steam" area on their way home from school, also a meeting point for mothers. It has been called "the Millennium Garden". It is appreciated by young and old alike and is a fine example of the strong community spirit of Colton residents.

The village hall committee decided that the hall needed to be extended, and more fund raising was embarked upon that enabled an extension to be added to the side of the hall and officially opened in 2006.

Another amenity for the village was also added to the church. A 'church room' was built in 2003 next to the church to house church community activities such as coffee mornings. The church has also run a well attended youth 'drop in' on Friday evenings. This is a good indication that St Mary's church is playing an active and important role in village life.

Also in connection with the church the early Tudor parish chest which had lain uncared for in the tower was rescued and is now undergoing careful restoration. A strong link with Colton's past parish history.

At the beginning of this new century it was decided to rebuild the bridge over Moreton Brook at the entrance to the village. This bridge had served residents for centuries but with the increased volume of traffic coming to and through Colton, it needed to take heavier weights. This was duly done and it was rebuilt to look just as had before complete with the ice age stones at each corner.

As this book went to print the new Rugeley bypass built to help ease the pressure of traffic coming through Rugeley, was

opened. It passes for some of its length through the parish of Colton again changing the landscape of the parish.

Finally on 12th October 2007 Queen Elizabeth II visited Colton in that she disembarked from the royal train at Trent Valley station in the parish of Colton on her way to Alrewas Memorial arboretum. The children of Colton school were there with many others to greet her. Possibly the only reigning monarch ever to visit the Parish.

Appendix

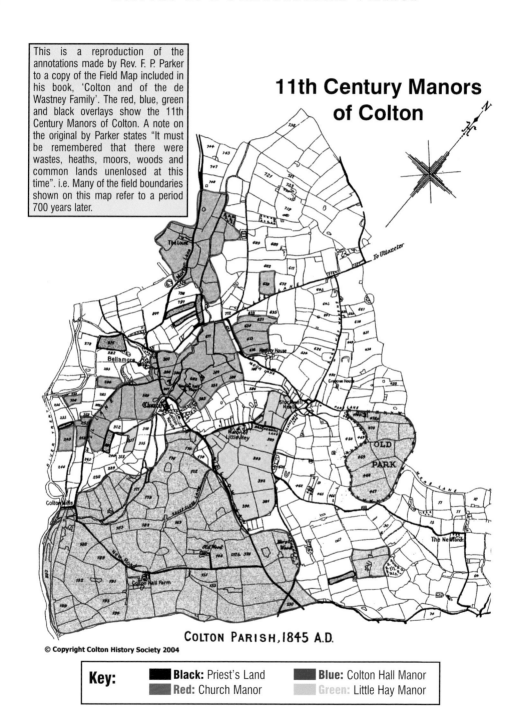

This is a reproduction of the annotations made by Rev. F. P. Parker to a copy of the Field Map included in his book, 'Colton and of the de Wastney Family'. The red, blue, green and black overlays show the 11th Century Manors of Colton. A note on the original by Parker states "It must be remembered that there were wastes, heaths, moors, woods and common lands unenlosed at this time". i.e. Many of the field boundaries shown on this map refer to a period 700 years later.

11th Century Manors of Colton

COLTON PARISH, 1845 A.D.

© Copyright Colton History Society 2004

Key:
Black: Priest's Land
Red: Church Manor
Blue: Colton Hall Manor
Green: Little Hay Manor

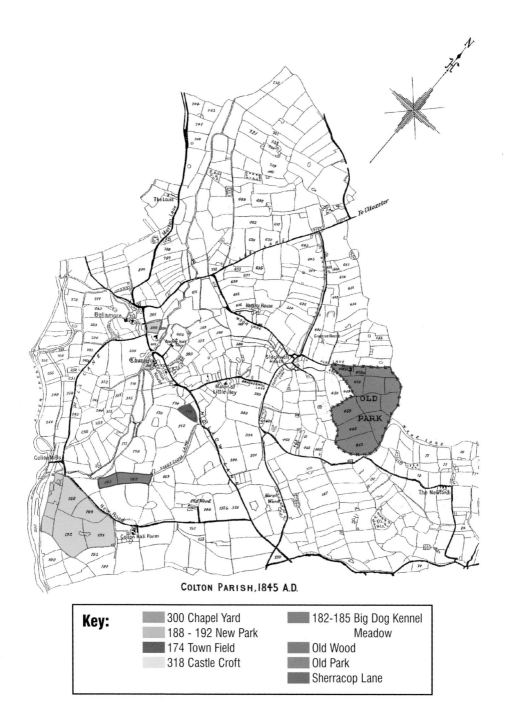

COLTON PARISH, 1845 A.D.

Key:

300 Chapel Yard		182-185 Big Dog Kennel Meadow
188 - 192 New Park		Old Wood
174 Town Field		Old Park
318 Castle Croft		Sherracop Lane

Names of Rectors of Colton through the ages as recorded by the Rev. F. Parker in his book 'Colton and the de Wasteneys Family'.

The symbol '*p*' identifies the person who presents them to the living of Colton i.e. appoints them. This certainly until the 1650's is the lord of the 'church manor'.

1086 A.D. Priest of Colton. Domesday Record.

1160	Gilbert priest of Colton
1203	Richard Parson of Colton *p.* Gerald de Colton (plea rolls)
1227	Robert the Priest, parson of Colton (plea rolls)
1254	John the priest (close rolls & 41 Henry 3)
1278 & 184	William de Beverley parson of Colton (plea rolls)
1303	Thomas de Bradewell *p.* Lady Avice le Mareschal
1307	William de Nostrefeld *p.* Lady Avice le Mareschal
1331	William Attewoode (plea rolls 4 Ed. 3)
1338	James de Runham *p.* Sir Robert de Morley. Marshal of Ireland
1340	William de Shulton (by exchange) *p.* Sir Robert de Morley
1342	William de Houghton *p.* Sir Robert de Morley
1349	William de Noble *p.* Sir Robert de Morley
1350	William de Hanley *p.* Sir Robert de Morley
1361	William Penne *p.* Sir John Gresley
1382	William Clerke *p.* Sir John Gresley.
1385	John Mayston *p.* Sir John de Gresley
1395	John Mellereth *p.* Sir. Thomas Gresley
1403	James Conyngeston *p.* Sir Thomas Gresley

1404	John Barston **p.** Sir Thomas Gresley
1407	John Russhebury **p.** Sir Thomas Gresley
1427	Henry Villers **p.** Sir Thomas Gresley
1431	Roger Hode **p.** Sir Thomas Gresley
1432	Robert Byrchore **p.** Sir Thomas Gresley
1441	John Thorpe **p.** Sir Thomas Gresley
1447	John F Flynton **p.** John Gresley
1451	Thomas Wolstote **p.** John Gresley
1460	Thomas Fleecher **p.** Sir John Gresley
1466	William Gresley **p.** Sir John Gresley
1470	Humphrey Brat **p.** Sir John Gresley
1499	John Gresley **p.** Sir Thomas Gresley
1500	George Tatton **p.** Sir Thomas Gresley
1544	John Wilson Sir **p.** George Gresley
1558	Thomas Tatton **p.** Sir William Gresley
1573	Roger Re **p.** Thomas Blunt and William Yate
1592	Christopher Hunt Rector for 59 years
1651	John Saunders **p.** Lord Aston
1683	John Taylor
1701	Samuel Spateman
1706	Richard Oneley **p.** Robert Landor
1708	John Taylor **p.** Rev. John Spateman of Yoxall
1738	John Taylor
1767	John Landor **p.** Robert Landor
1806	Charles Savage Landor **p.** Landor
1849	Abdeil Seaton
1874	Frederick Perrot Parker **p.** Charles Landor

COLTON WILLS

The following wills were transcribed by Shirley Carter for Colton History Society August 2004. They give examples of what two of the more wealthy residents of Colton in the 17th Century left in their wills. Thomas Yate was a yeoman farmer of some substance. His possessions are itemized room by room so we can tell from this what his house probably looked like. Anthony Bagot was a younger brother of Lord Bagot of Blithfield Hall and living at Little Hay Manor House. This manor belonged to the Bagot family.

(The use of the abbreviation Ms.illg. in the transcription of the will means that the word is illegible).

THOMAS YATE
March 25th 1642.
Lichfield RO B/C/11

In the name of god Amen I Thomas Yate of Coulton in the countie of Staffs, Yeoman though sicke in bodie yet being of good and perfect rememberance thanks be to god for the same do hereby make and declare this my last will and testament in manner and form following First and principally I commend and commit my soul into the hands of almighty god my maker; hoping assured through the merits of Jesus Christ my saviour to be made partaker of life everlasting And my body to be Ms.illg.

and Christian burial. Item for my goods whereas at the day of marriage if Isabell my wife I gave bond for the payment of a hundred pounds unto her for and in the name of a joynture in case she should survive and overlive me I do moreover give and bequesth unto the said Isabell my loveing wife one heifer and one colt. Item I give and bequeath and do hereby will and desire to the poore of the parish of Colton thirteen shillings to be distributed amongst them at the discretion of mine executor and the overseers of this my will. Item I give and bequeath to my daughter Katherine the wife of John Wildes of Stramshall twelvepence. Item I give and bequeath to John and Marie the two children of my said daughter Katherine ten shillings a piece Item I give and bequeath to my daughter Elizabeth the wife of Roger Wilkes twelve pence and to her daughter Marie ten shillings. Item I give to poor Sarah ten shillings. Item I give and bequeath to my son William Yate twelve pence. Item I give and bequeath to Isabell the daughter of William Yate five pounds. Item I give and bequeath to my son Henrie Yate five pounds. I give and bequeath to my son George Yate all my husbandry ware together with all my goods and debts undisposed of. Item I do make and ordain my said son George Yate sole and only executor of this my last will and testament. And I desire Mr Sampson Boughey and Richard Crispe (my loving neighbours) to be supvisors thereof. And witness that this is my last will and testament I have hereunto put my hand the five and twentieth day of March in the eighteenth year of the reign of our sovereign Lord Charles by the grace of god of England Scotland France and Ireland King defender of the Faith Anno Domini 1642.

Subscribed and published In the presence of Sampson Boughey, Thomas Yate Richard Crispe, His mark.

INVENTORY

The Inventorie of the Goods Cattles and of Chattels of Thomas Yate of Coulton in the Countie of Staffs. Yeoman

Deceased made and appraised by George Jeffrey George Butler of Coulton aforesaid Yeomen Hugh Bailey of Hamstall Ridware in the said Countie Yeoman and Simon Pedley of Coulton aforesaid? the 12th day of Aprill in the eighteenth year of the reign of our Sovereign Lord Charles by the grace of god of England Holland France and Ireland King Defender of the faith Anno Domini 1642

Imprimis In money together with his apparell	5- 0- 0
Item In Bills and Bonds	39- 6- 8
Item Three Silver Spoons	15- 0
Item land upon the park for one year	7-10

In the hall house

Imprimis Six brasse potts & two brass Candlesticks	2- 10-
Item four brass pans with a Mas	2- 0-
Item five brass kettles two brass skellets	
and two brass skimmers	16- 0
Item three tables with frames one form	
One dishboard two cupboards	
Together with chairs stooles	2- 6-
Item Two and twentie pewter dishes	
Three pewter Basone three flagons	
And other small pieces of pewter	3-5-0

In the great Butterie

Imprimis tenne potts of butter	
In the cheese parlour	2- 0- 0
Imprimis Six and thirtie cheeses	2- 4- 0
Item Twentie strikes of malt	3-0-0
15 strikes of blend corn	
20 strikes of barley	2-13-4
yarn	2-0
1 chest and 1 oldcoffer	10-0

1 pair of bedsteads   Ms.illeg

In the inner parlour

WILL OF ANTHONY BAGOT
18th June 1622

Transcribed by Shirley Carter – Colton History Society

In the name of God Amen. I Anthonye Bagott of Coulton in the countie of Stafford Esquire, Being sicke in bodye, but of perfect and good memorye thanks be given to god I doe make this my last will and testament in maner and forme, as follows First I comit and bequesth my soule unto the hands of Almighty God, hoping to be saved only by the bloode of Christ. Secondly I comitt my bodye to the earth to be buryed in Blithfield Church by my wife desiring such solemnization at my funerall, as myne Executors shall thinke meete. Thirdly as for my goodes, my will is that they bee soe disposed of according to former covenants, excepting thirtye pounds which I am indebted to my sister the Ladye Bromley which my will is it should be payed out of my goodes by my Executors and such other goodes as I shall by this my last will bequeath to others.

Impremis. I give to my three sisters Mrs Osbourne, Mrs. Oakover, Mrs Kinersley, three Duckits, which are in a box in my Cubbard with my evidences.

Item I give to my servants, as followeth: First to John Arnolde foure pounds, then to Anthonye Hunt three poundes, next to William Cowper three poundes, and to William Topping one pounde, and to Winifrede Dent three poundes, and to Anne Foaden three poundes, and to Elenor Sherbrooke one pounde, to Margery Milnor three poundes.

Item I give to the poore of Coulton two poundes to bee payed by my executors within a month after my funerall, within which time also my will is that my servants bee payed their legacies above mentioned.

Item of this my last will and testament, I constitute, and intestate my sister the Ladye Bromley, and my brother Walter Bagott of Blithield Esquire to bee mine executors, and given unto eyther of them an old angell, which bee in the forenamed box, hoping they will see this my last performed according to the trust, which I expect repose in them.

Item I give to my daughter a treble soveraign, and to my sonne in law a double Elizabeth soveraigne, and to my Grand child Katherine, the next best peice of gould which is in the same place. In witness whereof I put to my hand and seale, this 18th day of June ano Dom 1622

Lord? Baggot

In the presence of us under written Abdie Birch, Simn: Ash, John Carswell

WILL AND INVENTORY OF JOHANNE BATE dated 10th May 1578. LJRO
Transcribed by Shirley Carter – Colton History Society

In Doi none Amen the 10th day of May in the 20th year of our Sovereign Lady Elizabeth by the grace of god of England France & Ireland Queen Defender of the faith I Johanne Bate of the Lea in the Lordship and parish of Colton in the County of Stafford Widow being sick in body but of perfect & good memory. Do make this my Testament containing my last will in manner & form following. First I bequeath my soul to Almighty god my maker redeemer & sanctifier And my body to Christian Burial in the churchyard of Colton aforesaid. Item

I Bequeath to my masters Mr Richard Bagots wife my best tablecloth Item I Bequeath to Francis Lees my neighbours son one ewe sheep Item I Bequeath to Walter Woodward & Richard Woodward one ewe sheep between them., Item I give unto Walter Browne one ewe sheep. Item I Bequeath unto Francis Elton one lamb. Item I give unto everyone of my godchildren 2 shillings. Item I give unto every one of Richard Felkins children which he had by Jane Alsoppe 12 pence. Item I bequeath to every of Richard Walls his children 12 pence. Item I bequeath to every of John Ollyvers children of Rudgeley 12 Pence apiece. Item I Bequeath to Stephen Dyram of Colwich 12 pence. Item I Bequeath to Johanne Johnson my best mattress, my best coverlette. A double twill sheet a pair of sheets a bolster one voyder. A plain white towel a flaxen sheet my brass pan of six gallons. A flaxen kercheffe A flaxen apron a caste of Bees. A hempen bordercloth a flaxen muffler & 2 cushions Item I Bequeath to Joyce Hollingsworth a lamb one voyder and old coffer & a pair of canvas sheets. Item I Bequeath to Mary Dagett one lamb. Item I Bequeath to Mary Woodward one voyder. Item I Bequeath to Alice Brown Richard Brown his daughter one voyder. Item I Bequeath to Francis Aston his wife of Little Haywood my goddaughter my best voyder. Item I Bequeath to Thomas Sherbrooks three daughters of Coulley every of them a podinger Item I Bequeath to blind Johanne george one canvas sheet. Item I bequeath to Elizabeth Legge one canvas sheet & one single twill sheet. Item I Bequeath to Margaret Water 2 shillings. Item I give to Anne Sherbrook one yearling cow & calf one flaxen sheet a pair of canvas sheets a kercheffe a muffler a hempen tablecloth a coat & a smock. A coat to Agnes Sherbrook & one old black coat to Catherine Sherbrook her sister. Item I Bequeath to Raulf Bate & his wife my best bedhilling and one pair of flaxen sheets. Item I Bequeath to James Bate the younger 5 shillngs. Item I Bequeath to John Bate 2 shillings. Item I will that Raulf Bate shall have all my part of corne sown & unsown and malt also excepting such as shall be spent to bring me honestly whom at my burial & all part of haywain & of all other iron & wooden are & all my in store of household unbequeathed paying or allowing for the same to the performance of this my last will 30 shillings. Item I bequeath to Thomas Lees my neighbour a caste of bees. And where the aforesaid Raulf Bate hath heretofore bought my best brass pan for 10 shillings yet not paid my will is that he shall pay but 5 shillings for the same which shall be bestowed upon the poor by 12 pence a year yearly next after my decease as my overseer or some of them shall think most meet. Item I bequeath to George Webbe two shillings. Item I Bequeath to the church of Colton one flaxen sheet And a towel to Blithfield church. Item I bequeath to Roger Rowe parson of Colton 6 shillings and 8 pence Item I bequeath to Dorothy moore my velvet coat with sleeves & a kercheefe. Item I give to Anne Adcocke A flaxen apron & a flaxen kercheefe Item I give to Raulf Bates wife my second towel being of dyap a flaxen towel a flaxen apron my best kercheffe and my hat. And to Richard Browne his wife my best gowne being Lich meddeley Item I give to John Wright of Hamley gate one little brass pot and to his wife my workaday hat. Item I give to Fowell of Collwyche A twill sheet a canvas apron for his wife & to Thomas Partons wife a smock. Item I will there will be a good flaxen sheet cut in four parts and given at the time of my burial. Viz Mary Baddyley Jayne hatton Agnes Jaxon & Johanne gorse the widow & my body to be shrouded in a canvas sheet. Item I will that all the rest of my goods not before bequeathed shall be equally distributed among the poor of the parish of colton & Blithfield. Item I ordain make & institute my true & lawful executor Raulf Bate of Colton aforesaid to see this my last will performed as my especial trust is in him. And overseer of the same Roger Rowe clerk Thomas Lees and Richard Browne & these being witnesses John Bagott Roger Rowe clerk Thomas Lees Richard Browne John Hatton William Johnson and others.

The Inventory of goods and cattells of Johanne Bate Widow of the Lea in the parish of Colton taken the 24th day of October 1581 praised by Thomas Lees & Richard Browne

Imprimis the moytie or one half of three bullocks	
The other moytie being Raulf Bates	xls
Item the one half of one cowe & three heefers	xliiijs iiijd
Item in sheepe iiij cupples	xvjs
Item the one half of one mare	xs
Item the one half of ij swine	iiijs
Item in poultryr	vjd
Item in beddinge & napperyeware	xxxiijs iiijd
Item in arpell	xijs
Item in Corne sowen & unsowen, malte, Her parte of heye wayne & all other Iron & Wooden ware & suche in store of householde as is Bequeathed to Raulf Bate to the performance of the Will	xxxs
Item in brasse & pewter	xxs
Item ij castes of bees	vjs viijd
Sum	xli xvs xd
The Debts which are owe unto me Johanne Bate	
Imprimis in the hands of William ollyver of Rudgeley	xxs

Item in the hands of John ollyver of Rudgeley	xs
Item William Bate of Bagottts bromley	xxs
Item John hatton of newton	xxs
Item Elizabeth webbe of Stowe	xxs
Item William Johnson of Collton	xxxs paid hereof xs
Item Raulf Bate of Collton	xxs
Item John Woodward of Collton	xxs whereof I will that he shall paye

But xs in consideraon that I have bestowed a brasse panne upon my servante Mayde which in my former will I did beset to my neighboure woodwards wife.

As referred to in chapter 8 an extract from the will of John Webb dated 26. Jan. 1727.

"Item. I give to the churchwardens and overseers of the Parish of Coulton in the County of Stafford and their successors forever an annuity or yearly rent charge of 20/- to be issuing and payable out of my messuage house or tenement with their apportionment in Coulton aforsaid late in the holding of Ann Haywood widow upon St. Thomas's day yearly forever to be distributed on that day yearly amongst the poor of coulton aforsaid and at the discretion of the Minister of Coulton aforsaid for the time being."

(The tenement referred to was the Three Wheels Pub)

Lichfield Record office Ref B/C/11